More Praise for *Dying to Hang with the Boys*

"A story filled with courage and hope."

—Sue Abderholden, executive director,
National Alliance on Mental Illness (NAMI)
Minnesota

"This is intentionally not a story with a feel-good,
fairy-tale ending, but rather one that illuminates
and humanizes the myriad ways in which being
transgender can impact relationships, career
prospects, financial stability, and health. Readers
will find themselves rooting for Nate at each step
in his journey and gain insight into the subtle and
pronounced ways their own behavior can affect
the ability of transgender individuals to gain
self-acceptance."

—Ken Abrams, associate professor of psychology,
Carleton College

Dying to Hang with the Boys

a
memoir

Nate Cannon

SoulBalance
Press

Dying to Hang with the Boys: A Memoir
Published by SoulBalance Press, Minneapolis

To arrange for an interview or invite Nate to speak, email
runningrewired@gmail.com.

Paperback ISBN 978-0-578-43711-8
E-book ISBN 978-0-578-43715-6

Cover design by Brad Norr
Author photo by Wendy Zins
Page design by Beth Wright, Wright for Writers LLC

for my mom

Contents

Wake-Up Call

The night of my first slumber party, when I was six, I wore my boys' karate pajamas proudly. The girls greeted me with a mix of chuckles and sneers, compliments and questions. My mom had warned me: other kids were increasingly noticing my differences. Some seemed uncomfortable. Others curious.

I didn't care.

At the party I had to pretend to watch and enjoy *Dirty Dancing* before we finally got into our sleeping bags. I struggled to get comfortable and join in the whispering conversations. Eventually I fell asleep.

In the heart of the night, I awoke, jarred straight into sitting upright. I unzipped my sleeping bag, slid my feet to the carpeted floor, and tiptoed silently past the girls sleeping on the floor to the window. There I stood and stared out, mesmerized by the wind's shrieking ferocity as it bent the trees sideways, as if they were flexible toothpicks.

Something was wrong. I could sense it.

"Everything okay?"

I spun around to see Staci, another slumber party guest, standing behind me.

"Yeah," I said. "It's fine. Just can't sleep."

In the morning, the girls left one by one as parents and cars came and went. My mom had four kids to chauffeur around, so sometimes she ran late, but an hour went by, and she still hadn't arrived. I went outside with Lindsay, the host and my best girl friend, to kick a soccer ball as the last of the other guests pulled away. Soon after, her dad came out of the house and called me over.

"I just talked to your mom," he said. "She can't make it, so I'll give you a ride."

I WENT INSIDE and gathered my bags, loading them into his waiting car. Lindsay joined us for the ride. We pulled up the winding road that led to a small cul-de-sac where an A-frame house stood on a rolling Iowa hill. After one final curve, the only place I'd known as home came into full view.

It looked far different from the day before.

A blue tarp covered the roof. Shingles and debris, from paper to nails to insulation, littered the yard. The sturdy brick chimney had completely toppled over. A large, splintered tree branch pierced the neighbor's fence.

We crept up the driveway and around the small turn to park facing the garage. After getting out of the car in a frenzy, I stood frozen in the driveway, gazing at the destruction. The roof of my bedroom, peeled like bark from a tree, lay atop my stepdad's crushed car. I picked up a loose roof shingle and traced the jagged edges with my fingertips.

The hum of the garage door opening interrupted my dazed disbelief. My mom walked out to greet us. She calmly exchanged a few words with Lindsay's dad while Lindsay and I walked through the garage, sidestepping glass shard remains of the blown-out windows scattered over the cement floor. Time vanished as I walked into the house and headed towards my bedroom.

The room had bright yellow shag carpet, pale yellow furniture, and equally yellow walls. Not exactly appealing, but it was better than pink, which was the only other option my mom had given me. I'd embraced that room and the fact I could call it my own. My room was my escape.

My tennis shoes slowed to a stop as I neared the bedroom doorway. Beams of sunlight pierced the shattered ceiling, casting an eerie shadow on my safe space. With a few more steps forward, I could see that my bed was caked in dust and nail-studded shingles. If I hadn't been at that slumber party, I would've been in that bed.

I wanted to curl up under the covers and hide from the wreckage, but that was impossible. Speechless, I stared at the sky directly above me, the strips of pink insulation dangling from loose wood beams, the bed I could no longer see as my safe space. The comforting layers of security beneath those blankets had soothed the ache brewing within me. I didn't know if I'd ever find that security, or even feel at home, again.

1

Lost Boy

"I'm supposed to be a boy," I'd tell my mom each night as she pulled up the blankets to tuck me into bed. "I'm supposed to have boy parts." I meant this with confidence and conviction. But how does a five-year-old child know that? I certainly didn't pick it up at school or read it in any book.

I just knew. I always knew.

In my earliest memories, I was torn by the disconnect between the boy I knew I was and the girl I'd been assigned to be at birth. My mom once told me that while still in the crib, I played catch with my two older brothers. When my sister, the oldest of us four kids, tried to offer me dolls, I showed no interest. It wasn't that I couldn't accept myself. Instead I was being told society wouldn't accept *me*. In the '80s, in the heartland of Iowa, discussion of gender reassignment was almost taboo. Crying with my mom at bedtime was my main outlet.

It didn't stop my imagination, though. Up until puberty, I'd finish my shower and put on jeans, blast music, and stand in front of the mirror with my shirt off. I'd slick my brown hair back, stare at my flat chest, and sing, pretending to be the male singer of whatever band I was into that week.

As a social worker, my mom knew my gender differences would be a recipe for bullying. She thought she was protecting me from play-ground problems by asking me to be the girl she wanted me to be, but I despised every second of living as a girl. I had no choice but to let my sister brush and braid my hair because mom told me I had to. I wore the dresses mom gave me to wear to recitals. I conformed when forced, but my identity couldn't be suppressed.

Much as the toy stores suggested being a girl meant I should like certain toys, the teachers on the playground told me the pink bikes were for the girls and the black ones for the boys. I wondered who made up such a stupid rule. I didn't like the pink ones, so wearing my blue OshKosh B'gosh overalls, I walked over to the black Big Wheels and parked myself on one of those instead.

When my mom brought home clothes for me to try on, she'd ask me to wear the feminine ensembles just a few minutes longer. But I invariably felt a panicked embarrassment while wearing them and took them off as soon as I could, settling instead for the few androgynous pieces she'd allow me to have.

EARLY ON, BEFORE the consequences began to mount, my decisions posed more concern for teachers, parents, and coaches than for me. School was still a playground. After piano lessons, it was off to soccer or basketball practice with the girls or hockey or baseball with the boys. I sometimes wondered why I was the only girl who chose the sports the boys were playing.

I didn't want to wear a girly green outfit while baking cookies or knitting with a troop and their moms, either. I would've much rather have joined the Boy Scouts than Girl Scouts, but was told I couldn't. Not really understanding why I'd been rejected, I watched as my mom enrolled my brother John.

I didn't know about social inequality or the gendered hierarchy in our culture then, and I'm grateful for that carefree first decade of my life. I did normal things a normal kid does. For much of elementary school, and during the first year of junior high, what I now recognize as social injustice didn't faze me.

During the summer months, and when sports weren't in season, my friends—all boys—would often come to my house to hang out and ride bikes or rollerblade. I spent hours in-line skating and shooting pucks at a net on the vacant lot across the street. It became a perfect playground and place that, more and more, I could call my own. But it was in my corner bedroom, surrounded by music, hockey cards, and video games, where I felt most comfortable.

My music collection, known to my friends to be one of the coolest around, included a few odd ducks, like the *Pretty Woman* soundtrack. I didn't care much for the music, nor did I understand the movie the soundtrack came from, but something about the tape sure caught my attention.

It was the cover.

Propped up in her mini-skirt, knee-high boots, and hot pink halter top, Julia Roberts showed off her long legs and flawless figure. Like most young girls, I'd already gotten the message: Thin was in. Long legs were sexy. And that's what women should all aspire to. With my short, stocky legs, I knew I was no Julia Roberts. But that didn't mean I wasn't looking her up and down to see what I was missing.

One day my two best boy friends joined me to listen to music after we finished riding bikes. We sat, circling a collection of tapes and a boom box. I rifled through my collection, retrieved the soundtrack from the stack, and held it in my hands, fingertips still caked with dirt from the bike track. "I want to look like Julia Roberts when I grow up." My friends looked at each other and nearly fell over one another laughing.

"Yeah, right. You want to *look* like *her*?" Even my friends knew my aspirations to someday be a feminine woman were farfetched.

As my buddies shot awkward glances at each other, I stared intently at one half of the cover. "Someday I'll have that body," I murmured, dreaming of the day when I could feel as confident in my own skin as she seemed to be.

I know now I never wanted to be anything like Julia Roberts in *Pretty Woman*. I didn't want to look like her or even have her figure. I just plain *wanted* her. I recall women commenting on Richard Gere's looks when that movie came out. Much like the Big Wheels, I knew I was *supposed* to like the things deemed normal for other girls to like. But I didn't care. Fuck the pink Big Wheels. They couldn't compare. Just like he couldn't compare to her. I wouldn't realize it until years later, but Julia Roberts was my first crush. And for a long while thereafter I thought my attraction to women explained my gender differences, including my childhood desire to be a boy.

MORE AND MORE, I sought out places I could be alone with my imagination. In the summers, my family would spend a few weeks at a cabin in northern Minnesota. Every day I'd take my tackle box and fishing pole down to a dock set in the murky, marshy waters of an inlet.

Sheltered beneath the draping arms of a weeping willow, I found comfort in the solitude. A light breeze brushed the arms of the willow, wafting a light fragrance of fish and stagnant, muddy water. I turned to my tackle box and fishing gear. With bobber and hook in place, I pulled an earthworm from the soil of the bait box and threaded it on the hook, casting it out along with my anxiety. Like many young boys I knew, I was savvy with a rod and reel. They kept telling me I was a girl, though, and that I'd have to start behaving like one. Mom said I'd even have to start wearing a girl's bathing suit. I could think of nothing more mortifying.

I didn't want to be a girl, do girl things, or wear girl clothes. Besides, to be a girl meant I'd grow up to be a woman. And to be a woman meant I'd have boobs and a period, whatever that was. And I wouldn't be able to fish because girls didn't do things like play hockey or fish. But I didn't care what girls did. I liked hockey. I liked to fish. And someday, I knew, I'd grow up to be a real boy.

A PICTURE WOULD surface years later, a memento of a little girl in a boyhood dream. I sit on the dock, my straight brown hair cut as short as I was allowed at the age of six. I'm wearing my Michael Jackson-esque red jacket, stone-washed jeans, and white sneakers. And most notably, I'm smiling.

At the time of that photo I was still young enough to enjoy the freedom of boyhood. When I was alone, I often thought of myself as a boy in my head. It just felt natural.

As did sitting on a dock, smiling at the murky waters and silent surroundings, guarded by pine trees in the distance and reeds hugging the shoreline waters. I thrived on those moments where I could simply be the boy I wanted to be, hidden in a space where no one was looking and nobody could truly see.

2

Dislocated Identity

With sports in session and the fall coming along, I could no longer hang out with my boy friends. I'd join them for hockey in the winter, but I had to play basketball with the girls.

Though it was only fifth grade, winning the league championship felt like a big deal. We streamed out of the YWCA victorious and headed for the pizza parlor. I hopped in my mom's minivan, beaming with excitement.

"Mom, did you see that pass I made at the end? We won! This is awesome!"

My mom, all smiles, agreed. "It *is* awesome. I'm so proud of you!"

"Thanks. It's fun to be good at sports."

We both knew there was more to that statement. Something unspoken yet understood. My mom came to the game straight from her job at the hospital, still sporting her blazered suit. Snow crackled under the tires as she backed out of the parking spot. The other girls had crammed into a few select cars.

"Do you think you'll have fun at the party?" my mom asked. I stayed silent. "Well, honey, I worry the boys might not always want to be your friend, and I think it'd be good to try and get to know these girls outside of sports. Who knows, maybe you'll find you have some things in common."

"I don't think so, Mom."

I reminded her of a recent slumber party and how the girls watched chick flicks and talked about boys. None of that interested me; it just isolated me. I put my forehead in my hands to hold the weight of the memory. "I just don't fit in with them."

"This might be different. That was a slumber party." She reached over and patted my knee, prompting me to peel my head out of my hands. "They all seem to like you!"

"Yeah, but Mom, they're only nice to me because I'm good at sports. They don't want to be my friend." I looked out to the dark and desolate snow-whipped landscape, silent once more.

We arrived at the pizza party and took seats at the end of a long wooden table. Parents chatted among themselves as the girls gathered in small groups and then dispersed to play skee-ball and arcade games. Feeling like the fifth wheel, I played Pac-Man and then headed towards the restroom. Two teammates, Katie and Sarah, were exiting the door labeled "Women." Both blond-haired and blue eyed, Katie was the tall center, Sarah the power forward. We'd been close: they'd invited me to their slumber parties, and I'd invited them to my birthday parties.

The door swung open just as I approached. The girls stopped in the door frame, impeding my progress. "Hey," I said. "How's it goin'?"

Katie, already a good half foot taller than I was, put her arm across the door frame and smirked. Unsure what was happening, I took a step back. They giggled.

"Are you sure you don't want to use the *boys'* bathroom?" Katie said.

"Yeah, the *boys'* bathroom," Sarah echoed.

"What? No! That's gross." I shifted my weight, fidgety. Of all the girls on the team, these were two I'd called friends. Besides, I belonged in the girls' bathroom, at least according to my mom and my teachers.

"Come on, you want to use the *boys'* bathroom. Admit it!" Katie sneered.

"No, I *don't!*"

I tried to sneak under her outstretched arm, but Sarah blocked my path. The next thing I knew, I was pushed through a doorway. Panic overtook me as I looked up to see a urinal. Pressing the full weight of my body up against the door, I pounded my fist on the door.

"Lemme out of here!" The giggling on the other side of the door frame only increased my distress. I leaned harder on the door and pounded with all my might. It was a futile effort.

"C'mon Katie, Sarah. This isn't funny!" Tears clouded my eyes.

Abruptly, they let up their weight on the door. Tripping over my feet, I nearly fell through the door frame, regaining balance just in time to see them running the other way down the hall, laughing. I stood and stared. What just happened? Why would my friends do something like that? Was it supposed to be a joke?

THE GIRLS WERE starting to see that I wanted to do more than just do boy things. I wanted to *be* a boy, and the older we got, the more abnormal that was becoming. Just as my mom had feared, the kids were starting to see my gender identity as wrong. The ways I expressed my gender were far more extreme than what was deemed normal for a tomboy at that time. The late '80s and the '90s saw phenomenal growth for girls' sports, a field in which girls were allowed to display more stereotypically masculine behavior. Unfortunately, my male preferences and expressions of gender went beyond what society was yet comfortable with.

Craig, my oldest brother, told me, "You're a girl. You're gonna get boobs and have to start wearing a bra. You're gonna get your period. You'll need to shave. You just have to deal with it. You're a girl. Not a boy."

He was right. I detested learning about the menstrual cycle, puberty, and development, especially when it was reiterated what would happen to girls during puberty versus boys. Over time, one by one, each of the things my brother and the teachers said would happen to girls happened to me. But each time Craig or my mom, my teachers, my peers or their parents reminded me of what it meant to be a girl, I cried. And the more I received the message that my resistance to womanhood was wrong, the deeper inside I pushed my true feelings.

BY THE TIME middle school brought changes to both my body and the class schedule, the little boy inside me was becoming more and more lost. The expectations to be a girl were coming at me from every direction. It was hard enough to remember to cross my legs when forced to wear a dress. Now I was having to shower after gym class. The idea of undressing in front of the girls, especially those teasing me about my gender identity, was horrifying. All the love of sports in the world couldn't outweigh the shame brought on by having others see my female body. It was proof, in my eyes, that the onslaught of womanhood could no longer be hidden.

The body didn't lie.

I chose a gym locker away from the other girls, making any forced showers short so I could get out and put my precious clothes back on. It was as anxiety inducing as the thought of getting my *first period*, a fear I lived with for months before it finally happened. When it did, I broke down crying, alone in the bathroom, drops of blood staring back at me, apparent proof that my biological sex was taking over.

Mortified, I told my mom, who gave me the talk and a box of tampons. The thought of needing those was as embarrassing as the thought of having to try on my first bra: no matter what size or brand it was, it wasn't going to fit me.

Acutely aware of my turmoil, my mom brought home and discreetly gave me the feminine items I needed in adolescence. But she still demanded some control over my clothing. As I tried on A-cup training bras, my mom seemed to enjoy watching me put on a forced fashion show.

She believed she had given birth to a little girl, so that's what she wanted, or needed, to see. For her, that meant congruence. Seeing me in a feminine outfit seemed to make her genuinely happy. It brought her tears of joy to see me dressed as a girl. But inside I think she knew no dress or hairstyle or makeup would lead me to blossom into a feminine woman.

ONE BY ONE, friends drifted away from me. Like the locker room, the lunchroom became uncomfortable territory. At the height of my elementary days, I had a daily seat at the cool kids' table. By seventh grade, I was seeking out assignments from the office to avoid having to even enter the halls. The more isolated and excluded I felt, the more depressed I got. The more depressed I got, the more I looked like a loner. The more of a loner I looked, the further the kids stayed away.

The hockey league parents, just like the Little League ones, began having meetings about me. Puberty generated concern regarding the logistics of the locker room, road trips, and my safety. The boys were starting to hit their growth spurts, while I never did. I'd already sustained more than one concussion, and it was starting to take a toll on me. Still, I refused to let go. I continued playing with the boys, to the dismay of many parents. A private, curtained-off area became my own personal locker room. On the road, my dressing area often consisted of an old nurse's station or equipment room. At the time, I didn't mind. Not only did a private area prevent people from seeing underneath the clothes, but it kept me out of the spotlight of controversy. More than once, a mouse scurried by, catching the corner of my eye as I leaned over to tie my skates. I learned to pick up my bag and put it on a chair before I went out on the ice. Being alone, even surrounded by mice, was becoming more comfortable than being around the boys in the locker room. Mice wouldn't flash me, ask me if my boobs were getting in the way of my shoulder pads, or offer me their nut cup. And at least I was still allowed to play.

As ADOLESCENT HORMONES started to kick in, the social scene also began to change, and as is true for many transgender youth, my mental health started to suffer. Just going to school was becoming a challenge. Pretty soon I couldn't go at all.

I'd wake up, and if I could get from my bed to the shower, I'd maybe make it to the kitchen for breakfast. If I was lucky enough to do that, I might get in my mom's car. But by the time we got to school, my mind was racing as fast as my heart. The anxiety of wondering what might happen in the hallways and who might say or do what was exhausting. It swirled into a frenzy as my mom drove to the school and slowed to a stop in the parking lot.

It was becoming a pattern I couldn't break. Fears of further bullying and teasing were paralyzing every part of me but my tear ducts. I cried and shook, sitting in the parked car.

My mom tried everything she could to get me to go to school, but to no avail. I'd go home and go to sleep. I even stopped playing hockey. My mom eventually got me into the hospital for an evaluation. I was diagnosed with major depression, anxiety, and what was then referred to as gender identity disorder. It's what they now call gender dysphoria in the *Diagnostic and Statistical Manual of Mental Disorders*, or DSM, the book that can make you think you have sixty mental health diagnoses but that specialists use to diagnose patients.

The truth of my diagnosis, that I was transgender and they knew it, was not discussed with me. Instead, I was given a prescription for Prozac, therapy, and the instruction to return to school. I couldn't comply and ended up spending half of my seventh-grade year in a hospital program.

By eighth grade, I was working my way back into the classroom and onto the ice. Once the cruelties of middle school finally passed, high school brought a sliver of hope to my overall outlook, but it couldn't get me back in touch with my lost inner boy.

I EARNED A spot on an elite girls' hockey team in Minneapolis. My mom drove me there on weekends, five hours each way, solidifying our already unique mother-child bond. We sang along to U2 and Tom Petty and talked at length while sipping chocolate shakes.

I cherished the time we had together but found myself envious of the other girls. They all seemed so thin. My own weight had crept back up after I'd restricted my calories to the point of losing my menstrual cycle. Regardless of weight, they all seemed comfortable in the locker room. I loathed that puberty was turning me into a woman. They, on the other hand, seemed proud of their bodies.

But with my focus on hockey and school, I grew more confident in high school. I was being recruited to play women's college hockey, balancing my spot on the boys' roster with trips to Minneapolis to play with the girls. More and more, though, the brown, wavy locks crimped in a ponytail behind my helmet were becoming fuel for hostility when I skated with the boys. I drew unwanted attention and stirred controversy I wanted no part of—just by being a girl playing what was then still considered a boys' sport.

Some parents on the opposing teams even encouraged their sons to take shots at me. My mom heard the insults and threats as she sat silent in the stands amid the raucous crowd of hockey moms and dads. One night, as she tuned out the comments and focused her camera, I passed the puck up to my center from my spot along the boards and started skating up the ice. A blow across my mid-back halted my breath. The video shows an opposing player had hit me from behind, using his stick to check me headfirst into the boards. I put my arm up over my face and turned my head as I barreled into the unforgiving boards. My mom stopped filming, fearing the worst. The blow knocked me out and dislocated my shoulder.

It also took me out of the boys' world for good.

By junior year, I'd found a way to numb my pain—both physically and emotionally—through cocaine. As the months went by and it took more coke to get the same high, I began smoking crack. Pretty soon, I was going to any lengths necessary to get my fix. My mom tried everything to get me the help I needed as my high school graduation approached. In and out of treatment, I'd already finished my classes and was set to walk with my peers. I'd earned that right after all the years of schooling I'd put in.

But after being escorted into a psych ward, crashing off crack, and being ragefully depressed, I was given word I wouldn't be allowed to attend my own graduation ceremony. It was too much to process, too much to deal with. The drugs, my mental health conditions, the underlying frustrations. There was no escape from reality other than death itself.

A few days before I was supposed to graduate, I hanged myself. The attempt left me a bloody mess, my life forever altered by a complex brain injury and near-death experience.

It also rewired my brain.

3

Flat

Much of my late adolescence and early adulthood was spent wrestling with chemical dependency and mental health challenges or being confined to a place designed to help me with them. After an arrest and trips through treatments and hospitals, detoxes and psych wards, I'd had enough. I got myself into a program at age twenty-three and got myself into recovery. I started running, eating healthy, and listening to my body. I went back to school and finished my college degree.

I'd also thought I'd found myself within a lesbian identity.

Discovering my attraction to women explained—at least in my mind at that time—my gender differences. By college, I had no real awareness of my gender or even insight into how my gender was different during my youth. I just knew I liked women.

The locker rooms still felt uncomfortable, though, despite the fact some of my teammates were out as lesbian. Somehow the fear that my teammates could perceive me as looking at them in the shower paralyzed me from participating. I'd much rather have showered at home anyway. One teammate who was open and out was Krissy, one of the stars of the hockey team and an easy-going socializer who seemed to bring people together. We fast became friends, and somehow she ended up as my girlfriend.

Krissy and I grew close quickly, and she stuck by me when my darker side showed itself. She even got sober with me. We'd been together for six years when we bought a house. With over two years of sobriety, I landed a great job as a paralegal at a law firm to complement her advancing corporate career. But just months after I got my own career on the move, I developed dystonia, a neurological disorder closely related to Parkinson's disease.

In dystonia, the brain signal telling muscles to relax when not in use malfunctions. Sustained contractions then pull the body into abnormal and awkward postures. The pain and discomfort of what turned out to be a progressive form of the condition forced me to stop work as a paralegal after three years in the field. My neurologist told me that my chemical dependency coupled with my history of head trauma had rewired my brain.

The suicide attempt, along with all the chemicals I poured on the live wires after that injury, would leave permanent scars not just on my body but on my brain.

I kept on running, though, despite the discomfort and pain. With dystonia, I don't exercise to build muscle but, rather, to wear my muscles out. Sometimes that process can take hours. I intuitively knew I had to keep moving to manage my dystonia, just as I knew my correct gender as a youth. But in adulthood, I'd come to accept that I was born a woman even if I never really *felt* like a woman.

I believed that gender dysphoria stuff was all behind me.

One day I stared out the bay window to the well-manicured lawn of the house across the street from where Krissy and I were making our home. Another lesbian couple had recently moved in there. I wondered if they'd wanted to be boys when they were kids. If they'd been pushed into the boys' bathroom or got laughed at when they wore dresses.

A ferocious rumble rattled the plates in the cupboard, disrupting my introspection. When the wind hit right, we were in the direct flight path for both takeoffs and landings from the Minneapolis-St. Paul International airport. I seemed to be more sensitive to sound since the onset of dystonia. The airplane noise grated my nerves and amplified my irritability, which further strained my relationship with Krissy. What had at one time felt like perfection was beginning to fracture, mostly because of the limitations dystonia was imposing on me.

RUNNING SEEMED TO be my best outlet. Though I swore after my first marathon I'd never do it to myself again, the urge to reach that goal once again outweighed the dread of the difficulty. Krissy far preferred her bike to a pair of running shoes, but we had run a few short races together, and she wanted to try the challenge of a distance experience. We signed up for a half marathon set for the Fourth of July, which was to be a handy training race for my fall marathon. Despite the heat and difficulty of keeping a house up and working full-time, Krissy trained well and joined me on the starting line.

My dystonia was flaring up, though. I grimaced as I lay flat on my back on the ground, rain piercing my squinted eyes. The race that was supposed to be a fun bonding time was becoming a nightmare. I had wanted to push myself to race at a faster pace. But both my plan and the weather turned sour. Small drops that began at mile 3 grew more robust. By mile 5 I was drenched. And my dystonia, indifferent to the elements, didn't care to cooperate.

It swallowed me, starting in my neck and creeping down before triggering the abdominal and back spasms that had started earlier that year. In training for my second marathon, I'd so far been able to muscle my way through the runs, but it came at a cost. As throbbing spasms in my abdomen tried to buckle me at the waist, a set of hands seemed to latch onto my back muscles, grabbing me from behind and squeezing me like a dishrag, twisting my core and pushing my trunk forward. I was starting to resemble a hunchback.

Runners slogged by, swimming in humidity, heat, and an outright downpour. Several of them shot glances my way, evidently curious as to what I was doing with my back arched in the grass, rain pounding my face. In truth, lying flat is often the only way I can get the spasms to stop, even if momentarily.

I got to my feet and started again, trying to find my stride. Each time I did, the spasms crept back in. Inch by inch, mile by mile, I made my way forward. Dystonia, not fitness level, would dictate my pace and time from then on. But it couldn't get me to quit.

I eventually crossed the finish line and slouched my soggy self to a private area where I could lie down without a clock running. The ground beneath me, saturated from the rain still falling, enveloped my body. The pain took my breath away, rivaling that of my first shoulder dislocation. Despite my twisting, stretching, and arching, it clenched my muscles with raw, gnawing force.

From the corner of my eye I spotted a familiar face. "Krissy!" I rose to my feet as I called for her, but the dystonia buckled me forward. I physically could not make my body stand up straight. With hands on her hips and chest heaving, her smile vanished as she saw my pain and posture.

"Sweetie, are you okay?"

"I . . . yeah. My back and ab muscles are killing me, though." I tried again to stand up tall. I couldn't. "This is miserable. That *race* was miserable."

Krissy stayed silent. I took a moment to collect my thoughts. She seemed to need reassurance and compliments. "I'm so proud of you for finishing your first half, sweetie!" I didn't want my condition to take away from her accomplish or tarnish our memories.

We tried to hug, but my hunchback made it difficult. Krissy seemed to settle back in to enjoying her triumph, but I could tell my pain, my struggles, were straining the experience.

"I know!" Her blue-grey eyes lit up. "Let's go get our picture taken!"

Together we weaved through the throngs of people. Mostly she guided me as I struggled to stand up long enough to see anything but shoes and cement. The pain was consuming. It was all I could think about. But there's no time for pain when posing for a picture.

Side by side, arm in arm, we posed. She stood tall, straight, smiling ear to ear. I tried to match her expression and her posture but came up short, appearing slouched over with a forced smile. It would become symbolic of our relationship. I tried to be the pillar of perfection and project the image she wanted, but how I saw myself was constantly changing—whether she was in the picture or not.

My RUNNING STRUGGLES continued after the race. With the addition of Botox injected into my abdominal and back muscles, I made it through training and lined up for my second straight Twin Cities Marathon in the early fall. Lingering spasms persisted, again necessitating odd time-outs, when I'd run off the course and lie down to arch my back. But I finished—a great feat given my condition. I hid my pain from others, though. All they wanted to see were the accomplishments. They didn't see the struggles.

"Are you okay?" became a phrase I heard all too often. And all too often I had to lie, to spectators and Krissy alike.

"Yeah," I'd say. "I'm fine."

Everything was fine.

You can only push so much under the rug before you start tripping on it. My self-loathing and anger amplified as I wrestled more intensely with my gender. I hadn't felt that way since my youth. I didn't even recognize the feelings at first, let alone know what to make of them. All I knew was that suddenly those two 34B breasts sitting on my chest felt wrong. I'd feared them when I was a kid and was told I would grow them. I sure wasn't a bit happy at twelve when they first developed. But I'd grown into them, so to speak. I'd learned to accept that they were there; they were a part of me.

Now they felt out of place, as if they no longer belonged there—and never had.

I RETURNED HOME from a run on a warm fall day when only the wind reminds you the seasons are indeed changing, and, as usual, my back and abdomen were sorer than my legs. A hot shower was in order. I finished up, turned the nozzle off, and opened the shower curtain. Staring back at me was my reflection. Steam clouded the top of the mirror. The image was clear, though. It was a woman's body in the mirror.

"I'm a freak," I said aloud. "A fucking freak."

Towel in hand, I lifted each breast to dry beneath. My stomach turned. Why were these here? Why were they on me? Wrapping the towel around my waist, avoiding thoughts of what parts were missing down there, I stood silent, staring in the mirror at a body that belonged to me but that didn't feel like home.

Reaching up, I covered each breast with a hand to flatten my chest. As I did, my thoughts started down a circuitous track. I'd already cut my long hair off. Slick from the shower, it appeared shorter than it already was. It looked like a man's haircut. With my breasts concealed, so too did my chest start to appear like that of a man's. For a split second, I liked what I saw. A smile crept across my face. I *did* want the body of a man.

There was no doubt, though. The curve of the waist, of the hips; I was a woman, and nothing was going to change that.

Shame slapped me.

"Get over it," I said emphatically. "You are not a man. You do not want to *be* a man. You're a woman. A woman!" I was trying to encourage myself to embrace my identity as female, but more than that, I was trying to dismiss from my mind that I was even having such sick, devious thoughts. This sudden desire to be the other sex felt disturbing to me as an adult. It had felt so pure and natural as a kid.

I'd been confusing my sexual orientation with my gender identity for much of my adult life.

Towel still around my waist, I stared at myself. Cupping my breasts, then uncupping them, I'd imagine my body as that of a man's. Then my eyes would refocus, and all I could see were the curves of my figure, so feminine. It jarred me more with each passing second.

This couldn't be happening. I couldn't be having these thoughts again. I thought I'd put this away—far, far away—back when I was a tween. But here it was again, this pressing urge to change my sex. Only this time it wasn't as simple as it seemed when I was five. I could no longer tell my mom with innocent naïveté to "just fix it." She'd been right. It was far more complicated than waving a magic wand to turn me into a real boy.

This was psychologically devastating. Not so much the fact that I couldn't just go to the doctor and have it fixed, but that I was having these thoughts in the first place.

"Look at yourself. You're disgusting. You're a tranny, a freak." I stared, anger rising internally the longer I took in my figure. I couldn't outsmart my denial, though. I knew I was in that dreaded stage, just as I'd been with addiction, when I was trying to fight and simultaneously deny that I was struggling. That meant the struggle was, in fact, real.

Like addiction, I was preoccupied by my thoughts. Only, instead of drugs or alcohol, I was fixated and ruminating about my gender and body. With sobriety, stopping the thoughts of wanting to use comes from stopping the behavior of using. In that instance, abstinence is healthy. But in the case of gender dysphoria, denying myself the outlet of exploring my own gender identity was detrimental. It kept me in a closet. So in a polar opposite extreme from addiction, I had to allow myself to engage in thoughts and behaviors in order to get well.

All easier said than done.

"You gotta stop this shit. This is out of control." I stared hard into my own eyes, the looking glass through which I was now seeing myself. "Get it together and stop this nonsense. Now."

I had been disciplined in my recovery with respect to the governance of my own thoughts and behaviors. But this was beyond my control to abstain or refrain from. It was happening to me whether I liked it or not.

For months as I toiled internally with the dysphoria, outwardly I celebrated the progress I was making on my book. What others didn't know, though, was that my writing kept steering back to gender. The countless times I spent begging my mom to transform me into a boy. The times I spent isolated as a teen because I was too much a boy to be a girl but too much a girl to be a boy. The times in college, where I always had a weird sensation in the bathrooms and locker rooms, as if I were a guy hanging out in a woman's territory. I never felt comfortable dressing with the other girls, who seemed to have no qualms about socializing while half naked or showering together.

The struggle with dysphoria led me to look at and think about my own body. Not just look at it in a superficial way but really look at and acknowledge my anatomy. Eventually it dawned on me that I shouldn't have to pep talk myself into not loathing my female features. Dystonia was making it tough enough to love the body that was betraying me.

It had nothing to do with weight, so I couldn't attribute the body loathing to that. I was in great shape and proud of my fitness level and physique. No, this felt different from the battle with the scale I'd fought when I was younger. This felt like a raw, gnawing ache in my soul. It wasn't pounds but rather the defining biological characteristics of my womanhood that I wanted to make disappear.

Still staring, I snapped back to reality. The image in the mirror was becoming less clear. Water droplets were sliding slowly down across my reflection, distorting an already clouded image.

IN THE COMING weeks, as I was researching appropriate names to change the names of the people in my book, I realized I was also thinking about my name and what I would change my name to if I so chose.

For some reason, I kept landing on the name Nate. That reminded me of how I'd thought of myself as a boy during my youth, whenever I was out there alone rollerblading or riding my bike. Back then I thought of myself as a boy named Mark. So many of the memories being brought to the surface by my writing process were focused on wanting to be a boy.

Then there were the other urges. Along with cupping my breasts in my hands and pretending they were gone, I'd roll up a sock and shove it down the front of my compression shorts. I'd stand in the mirror and stare, wondering why I had these things on my chest and not those things in my pants. I couldn't wrap my brain around it. Me? A transsexual? The word is so powerful, so harsh. I couldn't process it.

But it was impairing every area of my life, from running, where I loathed having to wear a sports bra, to the times when all the layers came off. I couldn't even enjoy making love with Krissy anymore. My whole concept of my sexuality had changed. I was increasingly fantasizing about being a man while we were intimate. I couldn't stop the thoughts. I tried. I'd been having sex as a female for half my life. Why did this feel so unnatural?

I wanted to touch her intimately with male parts my brain thought I should have but my body didn't possess. I was getting the sensation of an erection. And increasingly, I didn't want to be touched in the ways she'd been touching me for years.

As the winter ushered in the cold nights, we nuzzled up together one evening and pulled the covers up over our sweaty bodies. She could tell something was amiss. I wasn't entirely present and spoke few words.

After an abnormally prolonged silence, Krissy sliced the air. "Sweetie," she said, tucking my short hair behind my ear, "what's wrong?" She'd been by my side for years. She'd endured my anger, eased my depression, dried my tears, and then held me tight.

Her brow furrowed once more. "What can I do to help?" She slid one leg over on top of me and rested her head below my neck.

"Nothing," I said, half under my breath, running my fingers through her thick hair. "It's not you. It's not you at all."

"What is it then? What's going on?"

This was not something I could discuss. Not something I could describe. It didn't seem normal. How could I ever explain this to her?

I didn't want to be touched like a woman any longer. I wanted to touch her as a man would touch a woman, but she still wanted to be touched by a woman. She also wanted to touch me as a woman would another woman. It was a sudden mismatch in our sexual desires.

We kept each other warm, wrapped tightly in one another's arms, as I fumbled to respond to her questions. Our mediocre but acceptable level of intimacy had grown to feel uneasy and tense. We'd been together for nine years. We knew each other's bodies as well as we knew our own.

I let go of the grip my toes had on the bed sheet to wrap my legs around her body, now pressed firmly on top of mine. We held each other cheek to cheek. The pressure of my turmoil squeezed until the emotion oozed out. Salty tears streamed down my face. I pulled my cheek away from hers, and we each turned our heads to look each other in the eyes.

I couldn't tell her what was going through my head as we lay intertwined. I couldn't tell her that, all of a sudden, after years of intimacy, I no longer could tolerate having my body touched the way she had been so accustomed to touching it. I couldn't say that I didn't want my breasts caressed. That I didn't want her inside of me. I couldn't explain that I wanted to touch her with a part of me that I didn't have and that she didn't want.

The distress, shame, and embarrassment bubbled up as the tears streamed down. Krissy delicately brushed each one away.

"I have something to tell you, but I'm afraid." The words, so guarded by my many defense mechanisms, slipped through my lips before I could stop them.

"You don't have to be afraid. You can tell me anything." Her near gasp for air signaled a level of concern from her I had rarely seen.

"I know, sweetie. I know I can tell you anything, and I trust you completely. This could change everything, though." My lip quivered as I fought the strain on my tear ducts.

"What do you mean, Jen? Please talk to me." She was practically shaking along with me. I rested my cheek on hers once more. The urge to burst into tears grew thicker as I let go of my embrace and looked up into her eyes.

"What would you say if I told you I thought I was . . . that I am . . . transgender?"

"What do you mean?" she asked. "Do you th—"

She paused, retreated from eye contact, and looked down seemingly at our breasts, pressed together. Krissy was well educated on LGBT issues. She knew the potential magnitude of what being transgender meant.

"Do you think you are?"

I hesitated as I looked deep into her eyes, slowly shifting focus from her left to her right. Our entire relationship seemed to flash before me like a kaleidoscope of blended images. The moment we met. Our travels abroad and long road trips. Getting sober. Running our first half marathon together.

As soon as the images collided, they vanished. Silence took over once more.

"Yeah," I finally exhaled. "I do."

The weight of my—at the time—self-perceived "sick" sexual deviance lifted off me. I'd said it. I'd gotten it out of me. I felt relieved, empowered by coming out. Then? Scared.

To my surprise, it all started to pour out of me. I told her everything, from the weird way I was researching names for my book, to stuffing socks in my pants and binding my breasts. I sensed immediately that she was struggling with it. She rolled over and lay next to me, her body almost rigid. Her whole identity as a lesbian had just changed. Suddenly, she was dating a man, and I found myself smack dab in the middle of a gender identity crisis threatening to take everything from me. She appeared almost uncomfortable. Her affect went flat.

She said she wanted to be there for me, but she wasn't all there from that day forward.

4

The Final Chapter

It appeared I was riding the high of my life. The memoir I'd toiled over for years was ready to hit the shelves, but nobody aside from my psychologist and Krissy knew what internal dissonance I was feeling. She showed her support by buying me a tie, addressing me as Nate, and talking with me about where I thought I might want to go with my gender transition. More and more, our conversation steered towards talk of surgery.

While I lived at home as Nate, on social media and to the outside world I was still Jen. The inner conflict intensified daily. Each supportive but gender-based message about my book stung deeper. "You go girl!" "You're such an amazing woman!" The praise only amplified my sense of isolation. It wouldn't get better anytime soon.

In mid-November, a historically disastrous month in my life, our insurance company denied coverage for the chest surgery it had initially approved. With the receipt of a single letter, the high I was riding was replaced by hopeless despair. Doctors were already hesitant to put me on testosterone given my history of brain injury. Now the chest surgery I'd worked with providers to get support for seemed out of reach as well.

This was devastating. I could no longer reconcile the person I saw in the mirror with the person I was on the inside. I felt like a rabid raccoon, caged, desperately clawing and biting to find a way out. It was starting to get dire.

I needed to transition. And it needed to happen immediately.

It felt just as urgent as any craving for crack or suicidal thought I've ever felt. I wanted to jump out of my skin, rid myself of my shameful affliction, and fix it through the easiest means. I wanted to slice my tits off with a knife I hated them so much. I loathed that they were there. How was I to proceed with taking on a male identity if I didn't look or sound like a man?

The more I ruminated, the more hopeless I became that transition would ever be possible. Dystonia would hold me back from testosterone. And insurance was never going to approve surgery, given its requirement that the person be living "full-time" in their preferred gender. Where, other than in the workplace, does "full-time" apply?

Even if I had been working at the time, did I really want to open myself up to the possibility of hateful backlash and discrimination? It's tough enough, as a woman transitioning to a man, to accept that you have a high voice, a feminine frame, and body parts only belonging to biological women. I was small enough that I could conceal those God-forsaken lumps on my chest. I could also dress like a man. Heck, I already did. But if you're not on hormones, it's extremely difficult to be seen as a man when your voice hasn't dropped. You feel as if you're trying to fool people, and it's an exercise in both frustration and humiliation. It's also a recipe for a hate crime. The requirement to live a year in the other gender was common among insurance companies at the time. They often required it to override the policy exclusion most plans had in place when it came to gender reassignment surgery.

It also felt like a catch-22. To get your name and gender marker changed, you needed to have undergone surgery. But to have surgery covered by insurance, you needed to be living in the other gender. Where's the logic in that?

It's tough enough transitioning to male. I can only imagine and empathize with transgender women, many of whom live their lives as females despite a husky voice and facial hair. Is it any wonder the suicide rate among the transgender population is disproportionately high? My legal background fueled my anger over this social injustice. I could hardly contain my rage as the urgency continued to squeeze my soul. The thought of having to live much longer as a woman was enough to make me want to die.

IN THE WEEKS after the book launch, my emotional stability crumbled. I detested promoting myself as Jennifer. Not only because that was the name on my book, but because I knew I'd risk losing some connections in the dystonia and lesbian communities if I came out as trans in a public platform.

I started a second Facebook account under my male name, Nate. There I was friends with Krissy and her family: the only people who knew my identity. I balanced that act as delicately as I did being Nate in my new email and Jen in my old email. Trying to be two people at once is a tricky act to keep up with. Sooner or later, you're bound to slip up. The real Nate was dying to come out, and the harder I tried to repress my male identity, the harder it was to remember to be Jen.

As November progressed, the rush of winter's chill wrapped the Twin Cities in a cold, grey blanket. With impeccable timing, as the most dreadful of seasons began to strip the life from the browning grass and barren trees, the long, drawn-out process for Social Security Disability came to a head as well. For almost two years, I'd gone to exams and sent in paperwork and finally was set to stand before a judge and plead my case.

Alone in my head, I had Krissy by my side. We braced against the cold wind and hopped on a train to downtown Minneapolis. I'd worked two years as a paralegal in an office just a block away from the Government Center. I'd spent countless hours milling in the courtyard while on lunch break, schmoozing with lawyers and other highfalutin, successful people. My past, before dystonia and dysphoria, was colliding with my present. I reached down inside my chest to force the oozing sections of my breaking heart back into place. I knew then the verdict would not be favorable. And that even the government thought me to be capable of very little.

Krissy squeezed my hand, pulling me back to reality as the judge released us. I bolted out of the courtroom to the elevator and pounded on the down button, as if doing so would expedite its arrival. With Krissy on my heels, I made it to the ground floor and hurried outside to the courtyard. Next to the elaborate water fountain, frozen over by the season's change, I came unhinged. Eyes followed from every direction as I sobbed. Krissy reassured concerned onlookers. "It's okay," she smiled.

It was always okay.

We talked the next day at home, and she seemed to understand why I was frustrated. She assured me we'd be alright. The financial aspect of our relationship was already complicated, and ever since I'd been unable to work as a paralegal, I'd been able to contribute less and less to our finances. But I was growing weary of her words. I didn't buy that she was happily supporting my not being employed while working her tail off and going to school for her MBA. I didn't believe she was okay with how much my condition was costing us.

Then there was the dysphoria.

I got up from the kitchen table and went to the other side, putting my hand on her shoulder. She stood, and we fell into a prolonged embrace. Forever stoic, Krissy shed no tears.

"I love you, Krissy. So much. But dystonia, gender—it's coming between us. I want to believe what you said in your email the other day. I want to believe we may have our individual struggles, but together make the strongest team around. It's just that sometimes I think you'd be better off without me in your life."

"That's nonsense." She pulled back to look me in the eyes. "I'm not going anywhere. I love you, and you aren't asking too much. There's no price tag on your happiness, Nate."

"There's not?" I peeled away and paced the kitchen. "How are we going to afford surgery *and* my dystonia treatment?" She stayed silent. "We shouldn't have to pay for this out of pocket. Even if Garramone *is* the best surgeon in the world for this procedure, we shouldn't have to pay for something that's medically necessary."

"He gets amazing results, Nate. They look way better than the U doc's. You're only doing this once. If insurance won't cover it, then let's have it done by the best."

My insides felt conflicted. On the one hand I was so grateful for her words that I wanted to kiss her hard and take her straight to the bedroom. On the other hand, I felt like a burden. Perhaps it was this mix of anger and irritability, all overlapping with hopelessness, despair, and constant, pressing suicidal thoughts that were fucking with my head.

It had to be something other than depression.

IN THE DARKNESS of my mind, I couldn't believe she'd be willing to spend so much money on me. My thoughts spun the conflict into an outright emotional storm in my head. Something told me that underneath her words, she was none too happy with how expensive I was. Still, we were partners. We may not have been able to make the vows in a formal sense, given that same-sex marriage was not yet allowed, but in our hearts we had. We were in it for better or worse, in sickness and health, for richer or poorer, 'til death do us part.

Those traditional wedding vows suggest you ought to be there if the other person encounters health setbacks that impair their earning capacity.

A few weeks later, on a Sunday, I awoke early as usual and prepared myself for a run. For some reason, I only ran a few miles. At least that's what my GPS records show. I don't recall a thing about the run. Nor do I recall what happened when I returned home.

I do know Krissy and I got in an argument. I have no idea what about, but according to her and my mom, I got quite angry.

She walked out.

I melted into a puddle of sorrow as she closed the door, headed out for "a walk." I knew it was over. An eerie silence overtook the house. Not even the incessant buzz of the airplanes taking off and landing could fill the void. My brain went into mass chaos.

I had to escape. From my brain. My body. My situation. From the charade of pretending we were living a life happily ever after when I knew in my heart of hearts that it was all just a ruse. Krissy didn't want to be with a man. She supported my transition and said she would love me regardless of name or anatomy, but my changing gender identity was changing her sexual orientation. That was a fact she was not yet willing to deal with.

And I knew she wasn't okay with the expense of my conditions. The dystonia alone was costing thousands out of pocket each year. To add gender reassignment cost on top of that was too much. This was all too much.

I paced the main living room.

Bright and airy with hardwood floors, it was the first room we saw when we viewed the house before we bought it. It's where we entertained what few guests we had. It was also the place where we displayed pictures. On the mantel of the fireplace was a beautiful shot of the two of us, taken just four months earlier. Against a stunning white background, Krissy sat behind me, arms wrapped around my waist, lips pressed against my cheek. The natural smile creeping to my eyes matched hers. We looked in love. And we were—on the surface.

I grabbed the frame and removed the picture. From the bedroom I grabbed the skinny black tie Krissy had bought me and with the two items in hand, locked the doors, picked up a pen, and headed downstairs.

In the corner, next to my PT equipment and weight bench, was the treadmill we purchased soon after we bought the house. It was a symbol of my running endeavors: a piece of machinery that had taken on a life of its own as a tool for maintaining sobriety and mitigating the symptoms of my dystonia and mental health conditions. I looked down to my hands at the other symbolic piece of the puzzle: the tie. It represented my gender transition efforts and setbacks. I'd been too ashamed to ever wear it. But there it was, a tangible symbol of Krissy's encouragement of me to be my own man, coupled with my own shame.

I clenched the tie tight with my left hand as I shifted the pen to my right. On the picture, a reflection of ten years of love we held together, I wrote words I don't recall writing, but that were later described to me. To this day, they disturb me.

With the epitaph of our relationship scribbled on what was as important to us as any wedding picture, I kneeled and began wrapping the tie in a knot around the bar of the treadmill. Memories of my suicide attempt at age seventeen flashed through my mind. There would be no snapped electrical cord this time. And there sure wasn't going to be any knots in the tie coming loose. This was going to get done right.

The knots were in place, but a knock boomed on the back door at the top of the stairs.

I hurriedly took the tie and began wrapping it around my neck. One loop would do. It was the knot I was concerned about. Still unsure how to make a slipknot, I tied the tie as tight as I could, cinching it to compress my neck as much as possible without losing consciousness. I had to make sure the knot was secure before I let go and let the light take hold.

Another bang on the door. "Just a second!" I yelled.

The banging stopped. There would be no further sound. Knot tied securely, I tested it for strength. On my knees, with my body facing away from the bar of the treadmill, I leaned forward. The tie stayed secured. My tongue began to thrust upward from the clenching wrap of the tie. The pressure behind my eyes and in my head intensified as I could feel the oxygen starting to struggle to exchange between my heart and brain.

It was time to write the final chapter.

I leaned forward and let my arms dangle. The pressure of the tie squeezed against my neck. What little air I was able to obtain before was no longer reachable. The tie was cutting off all oxygen, just as I hoped. Red panic flashed through my sight before a calming white sheet blanketed my vision.

I closed my eyes. And let go.

5

Rude Awakenings

I opened my eyes to foreign surroundings. I sat straight up in bed, startled by the realization that I had no clue where I was. I looked down to see I was wearing a hospital gown and attached to a multitude of wires. I looked up to see a whiteboard in front of me with the name Nate on it and a few notations of observations made on me.

What the hell? How'd they know I was going by Nate?

The fog lifting, I started to piece together clues to where I was. To my right were windows. To my left sat Krissy and our very good friend Marie. They'd been friends for years before I ever entered the picture, but Marie and I had become close and realized we had much in common with our tendencies towards anger, addiction, and self-loathing. With her long brown hair tucked up under a baseball cap, Marie sat silent as I attempted to absorb the shock of my whereabouts.

"What the fuck?" I turned and looked at Krissy. "You outed me? To Marie and everyone?"

I was pissed. And more than that, I was convinced I was pissing my pants.

"Why does it feel like I'm wetting the bed? What the hell is going on? How did I get here?" None of this made sense. Tried as I might to recall the events that put me in this now precarious position, I had absolutely no recollection of anything leading up to where I sat. All I knew was that I seemed to be in a hospital room, attached to gizmos, staring at my not yet legal name on a board. I was deeply shamed.

As much as I loved Marie as a friend, and for as much as we could relate, I could never bring myself to tell her about my transgender feelings.

Even though she'd had another friend transition many years prior, she'd commented often about how more lesbians are thinking they're trans now just because they have fleeting moments of wanting to have a dick for sex or thinking it would be easier to be a man in our society.

I was already risking alienation for coming out from two of our best coupled lesbian friends, Molly and Maureen. I couldn't afford to lose all my lesbian friends at once.

Two nurses rushed in, realizing I was conscious and conversing. Vitals were monitored; questions were posed. My responses stayed short and curt. I still had no idea what was happening and wasn't about to trust poking, prodding nurses treating me for something I had no memory of.

My simmering anger finally boiled over. The lack of control, the not understanding, the fact my partner had informed our mutual best friend of something I'd intentionally held off on telling her about. I again lashed out at Krissy. The nurses intervened and began questioning me further.

"Hold on, hold on now. Do you know why you're here?"

"No, I don't," I said. "Do tell."

"Do you know where you are?"

"Well, by the looks of it, I'm in a hospital. It also appears I've been outed. And does it matter to anyone that I'm sitting here in a puddle of my own piss? I swear I've wet this bed."

"Can you tell me your name and the year?"

"It's 2011. And of course you'd have to ask my name. Board says Nate, doesn't it? But my legal name is Jennifer. Jennifer fucking Cannon. Tell me why I wet this bed!"

"Who is the president of the United States?"

"Good God. Barack Obama. I asked you a question."

The interrogating nurse stepped out while the second continued her Q and A. Eventually she peeked under the covers. "I assure you you've not wet the bed. What you're feeling is the catheter."

"A catheter? Why? How did I get here? How long have I been here?"

The nurse paused from jotting notes and looked at me. "You attempted suicide. Almost a week ago," she said.

I took a moment to try to process this news. "Okay . . . and what exactly is your role here?"

"I'm one of the nurses caring for you here in the ICU. My name is Marge." She returned to jotting notes.

This couldn't be right. What was she talking about? ICU? Memories of my suicide attempt at age seventeen crawled through my brain. But despite scanning the channels of my every brainwave, my memory held no information regarding any recent suicide attempt.

"What did I do, Marge?" My shaky voice was now barely audible.

"You hanged yourself," she said.

She reached over my body to adjust the wires and removed a nasal tube that had been administering oxygen. "You're very lucky to be alive. You went into complete respiratory failure and were placed in a medically induced coma. We weren't sure you'd come out of it, but you're a fighter! There must be a plan for you here on Earth. Your work is not yet done." She drew up the corners of her mouth in a smile and cocked her head.

"Well, why did I survive? If I attempted suicide, I certainly wasn't going to allow room for failure."

Marge looked at Krissy, then back at me. "Well, your partner saved you. She did CPR and called 911."

MUCH LATER, I learned that at the time the EMTs arrived in response to Krissy's 911 call, I was down to four respirations a minute. Average respirations per minute for a healthy adult are between twelve and sixteen. My vitals continued to deteriorate as the ambulance approached the hospital. Had no further intervention been taken, I would have succumbed to my injuries despite the resuscitation. As it was, by surviving I was at risk for severe brain damage.

A medically induced coma allowed the doctors to regain control over a situation that was rapidly spiraling. By simultaneously inducing therapeutic hypothermia, they attempted to preserve functioning of my brain and heart.

There's no question I stopped breathing. Krissy did not find a pulse and believed my heart had stopped as well. Though she got me breathing again, the lack of oxygen was still challenging my respiratory system. ER notes show that fluid was starting to build up in the lining around my lungs.

Things got worse in the ER. A coma was my best bet not only to come away alive and breathing, but to speak and communicate as well. My prospects for recovery were uncertain, and I showed myoclonic jerking upon regaining consciousness, which was noted as "concerning" for hypoxemic brain injury.

Another brain injury was the last thing I wanted. I didn't want to be saved at all.

I'd wanted to die.

I DON'T RECALL much from the weeks leading up to the attempt, but I remember that the suicidal thoughts had gotten very pressing. The Social Security Disability hearing, the incongruence between my feelings of my gender and how the world was viewing me with my book out, the fear of losing everything I was building if I were to come out, the fact that surgery was approved and then that approval reneged. It was all too much.

I looked over from the bed once more to see Krissy sitting eerily quiet, her chin trembling. Marie was sobbing. She doesn't cry often, and Krissy never does. This was a big red flag.

What was I missing? I survived, despite my wishes, so shouldn't they be happy? Yeah, I was pissed off. Waking up in an unfamiliar place and not knowing how you got there could do that to anyone. It only made matters worse that I'd just awakened from a coma, which can trigger angry responses in some people.

I laid my head back flat. I knew something was different. Just looking at their faces I could tell. The air felt as thick as the forced breaths I'd been taking through the tubes implanted in my body. *If I had only taken that health care directive to the bank and had it notarized,* I thought, *she would have never been able to perform CPR, and they would have never been able to intubate me.*

I'd screwed up again.

I tried snapping out of the thoughts spiraling around my head, but I couldn't. I certainly wasn't being a very good host to my guests.

Marie said very few words while in the room. According to my mom, Marie broke down crying when she stepped out of the room. My mom had flown in from North Carolina, where she'd moved from Iowa in 2006 to start a new life with her new husband. This wasn't exactly the trip to Minneapolis she was hoping for.

There I was: scared, angry, confused about being conscious. And the people I'd loved most in the world seemed unwilling to talk to me about something I couldn't quite put my finger on.

After Marie and Krissy left the ICU, I had just one other visitor: Brian, whom I'd met in a writing class. He arrived just as hospital staff entered to do cognitive testing on me. He had no idea I was transgender, but when the nurse addressed me as Nate, the cat was out of the bag. As if the name on the board wasn't enough. I came clean, and he was more than accepting. He sat idly by during the tests. To my surprise, I scored quite well. But he could see, as I could, that I had really come close to losing my life.

Apart from Brian, my mom was the only one to come see me. After that day, Krissy never visited the ICU. Neither did her mom, who had also flown into town. Another red flag.

Hooked up to wires, and still nauseous from the anesthesia, I struggled to keep food down. All I wanted to do was sleep. The hours blurred into days. I'd wake up, and a nurse would enter with a tray. "Breakfast time! Pancakes, eggs, toast, fruit, and orange juice." I'd eat. Then throw it back up. Another nurse would enter. "Your potassium is low," she'd say, handing me a glass of orange liquid that looked nothing like orange juice and tasted more like floor cleaner. I'd swallow it down, but it too churned in my stomach. I'd vomit more. I'd try to eat. I'd vomit more. "Your potassium is low again." It was a phrase I got all too familiar with.

For days this cycle repeated as I fought to stabilize my electrolytes. I remained hooked up to machines, on one-to-one surveillance. A young woman in her early twenties sat in a chair at the foot of my bed doing homework. She was basically there to keep an eye on me, to make sure I didn't hurt myself again.

At some point, I began to long for the clean feel of a warm shower. I'd gone out for a run the day of the attempt. I came back and promptly tried to kill myself. Though I don't remember all the details, I know I hadn't showered or even changed my clothes before the suicide attempt. I certainly wasn't given any shower or bath when I was comatose. Some time later, the compression shorts I was wearing during the attempt were returned to me in a red biohazard bag. I'd voided my bladder and bowels during the attempt. Such a glamorous thing hanging is.

Feeling full of sweat, blood, piss, and shit, I asked the student if I could shower.

"Well . . . yes, you can," she hesitated. "I just need to be in there with you."

This would be awkward and upsetting to anyone, not just someone transgender. My medical records still said I was Jennifer and female. Most of the staff seemed to struggle to understand what I was experiencing. Some would address me as Nate, then refer to me as "she" or "her." Others called me Jen, even though Krissy asked them to call me Nate and refer to me by male pronouns. Sure, in the process, Krissy outed me to the people I was most concerned about telling, but since everyone knew now, what else did I have to lose?

I turned to the student as she spun her long brown hair into a ponytail. "So . . . you have to come to the shower with me?"

"That's right," she said.

"Do you have to, like, be *in* the shower with me?"

"You have to remain in my eyesight."

"This makes me really uncomfortable." My eyes cringed at the thought. She saw my discomfort.

"Why is that?"

"Well, because I'm transgender and you're female and I don't know that I'd be any more comfortable with a male but the fact is that this body—the body you'd see—is not . . . it doesn't belong to me, okay? And that doesn't make me feel very good about myself."

"Well, it's something we have to do. It's protocol. You're on one-to-one suicide watch while in the ICU, until you get up to the psych ward. So that's what we need to do if you want to take a shower."

I relinquished the fight. "Very well."

After the student and a nurse unhooked some tubes, and with the hospital gown undone in the back, I sat up from the bed, having surrendered my war against involuntary overexposure.

"Careful standing up," the nurse said. Sure enough, lying flat for weeks makes adjusting to an upright posture a bit of a challenge. As I caught my equilibrium and began to take a step forward, the muscles in my legs reminded me they hadn't moved recently, either. The dizziness and stiffness lingered as I wobbled my open backside to the shower. There I removed my gown and got my first glimpse of my bruised and aching body. I noticed cuts up and down the outside of my left arm. I don't remember cutting myself. I never took to cutting. But I had dug deep and left some permanent marks. I tried to scrub gently over them to prevent them from opening back up. I lathered and rinsed, washed and scrubbed, and at the end of the shower, we returned to the room.

Thankfully, they had taken the catheter out, so I no longer had to worry about that feeling I was peeing the bed. For as intensely uncomfortable as I was with my body at the time, the last thing I wanted was an object inserted in a part of me that was unquestionably female. That part of me wasn't supposed to be there in the first place. If it hadn't been for that part of me, I wouldn't have been standing in that shower. In fact, I thought, if it wasn't for the fact that I was assigned female at birth, this suicide attempt wouldn't have happened.

The closet was literally going to kill me.

I DON'T REMEMBER much of anything following the shower until I got up to the psych ward. I don't recall how I got up there, either. I don't remember any wheelchairs or elevators or hauling of any belongings. All I know is that I arrived. And not too long after that, so too did Krissy.

My mom had warned me that Krissy might not want to be in our relationship anymore. It didn't sink in. "She'll come around," I told her. "I'm sure she's just traumatized and scared by this. I'll talk with her and give her all the space she needs."

She entered through the double set of locked doors wearing a beige sweater and what appeared to be a fresh haircut. She was carrying a paper bag with items I'd asked her to bring me from home. I smiled as I approached her.

"Hi sweetie, it's so good to see you. Happy anniversary!" I reached up and wrapped my arms around her. Her embrace felt unusually vacant, and she didn't want a kiss.

"Your hair looks really nice," I told her. She began walking down the hall towards the nurses' station. "When did you get it cut?"

"Over a week ago." That would've been before the suicide attempt. But the days and weeks leading up to that attempt were now nothing more than a hole in my memory.

We walked down the hallway, dropped my stuff at the nurse's station to be searched, and went to the room they had assigned to me and me alone. At least they got that part right. They didn't try to put me in a room with a female. They didn't risk putting me in a room with a male. They didn't know where to put me, so they gave me my own private room.

What a luxury. A suite in the psych ward.

It's a tough thing to have to work with transgender people in a hospital setting when they are still living in the gender they don't want to be. The medical records must reflect the legal name and gender, and, of course, the way people are matched with roommates is dependent on those facts. As such, it creates a weird dynamic when you're a trans person on the psych ward, potentially taking up a bed that would otherwise be occupied by someone else in need.

Krissy and I walked in and sat down on the thin mattress. I nervously tugged at the sleeves of the maroon sweatshirt I was wearing, one that Krissy's mom had bought me as a gift many years earlier.

Krissy didn't seem quite right. She was quiet, almost sullen.

"Is everything okay?" I finally asked. "You don't seem like yourself."

"I . . ." She hesitated and started to tear up. She took hold of my hand. I wrapped my other hand around hers. Her eyebrows quivered as she locked my stare.

"I . . . I can't do this anymore. I need to leave. To get out."

"Get out? What do you mean? Of the hospital?"

"No . . ." she shook her head. "That's not what I mean."

"Listen, I know this had to be terribly traumatic for you." Some deep internal sense of panic was starting to rise up and engulf me. I really scared her. And probably scarred her. "I'm so sorry, Krissy. I never meant to hurt you that way. I don't even remember what hap—"

"No . . . please . . ." she said. "Stop." The tears started to stream down her face. She looked down, sighed, and collected herself before connecting her piercing blue-grey eyes with mine once again. "I need to get out of this relationship."

I couldn't find the words. My jaw went slightly agape as my wide eyes scanned the room before coming back to attention. "But I . . . I survived. I'm still here. I'm ready to turn a corner. I know this was tough, but I see now that I need to move forward with my transition. I can do this. I know I can. And once I do, I'll be a much, much happier person."

Krissy raised a hand to her eye and wiped a tear away. "I'm sorry. This was a decision I had to make when I walked out of the house that day. I knew I had to go. But this was a long time coming."

"A long time coming? Are you sure this isn't the trauma talking? I know this had to be awful to go through, and I feel horrible. But we're a team, right? We can get through this."

She shook her head slowly as she fished a tissue from her pocket.

I was trying desperately to absorb everything she'd said in so few words. It wasn't working. I didn't know what to say. I pleaded with her to stay while simultaneously telling her I respected her decision to leave. I tried to get her to stay while encouraging her to fly free. I babbled on and tried to rationalize things before my emotions overwhelmed me once more.

She said absolutely nothing.

We soon sat silent together, crying, nothing but grief circulating in the air. Eventually she reached over and gave me a hug. "I have always loved you, Nate. You are an amazing person, the most amazing person I've ever known. I wish you all the best in your future. But I need to leave. I need to go now."

How could this be happening? How could this be? I couldn't be losing my partner. It was our ten-year anniversary. Why would she choose that date to break up with me, especially if she felt it was a long time coming?

"I don't understand, Krissy. Why can't we work on this? You've only come to one therapy session with me. I'm trying to work through all of this gender stuff and everything else with the dystonia and my family and everything. And you seem to want me to go through this journey alone. I can't do this alone. This impacts you too, and you told me you'd stick by me, that we'd get through this together. Can't we give this a second chance? We can make this right, sweetheart."

Her stoicism flushed back her emotion. "I'm sorry," she said. "My mind's made up."

She stood up from the bed and pulled a piece of paper from her pocket. She unfolded the letter and described to me what she saw when she found me unconscious and not breathing. My eyes were bulging; my tongue was swollen. My face was purple and my eyes bloodshot. It was a gruesome picture of a lifeless body that she had to revive before the paramedics arrived. A traumatic experience that will stick with her forever, I'm sure.

We got up together and walked to the door of the room. I followed her down the hallway, which seemed to shrink with each passing step. She pressed the paging system to request the doors be unlocked. I folded my arms in front of me and propped one up on the elbow, covering my mouth with my hand to prevent the emotion from screaming out of me. I managed to pull it together as the doors began to open.

"I hope you'll reconsider, but I respect your decision either way. Think it over. I'm willing to give you as much time and space as you need."

She looked back at me once more with a hollow stare.

"Good-bye," she said. The gated doors creaked steadily across their track. Her face, her eyes, and her body slid slowly out of my sight until the doors closed completely.

She was gone.

6

Shocked

I picked at the vanilla ice cream in the tiny Styrofoam cup and swallowed a spoonful. I was tired of wearing scrub pants and the maroon sweatshirt that reminded me of Krissy's mom. Tired of wrestling with my gender. Tired of trying to process the thought that the last time our lips would ever touch, she was using the air in her lungs to breathe life into mine.

My mom was visiting me that day. "Sweetie, this breakup is gonna take quite some time to process. Maybe this isn't the right time to change your gender. Maybe you should wait on that awhile until things settle down." Of course her words were well intended. She really wanted what was best for me and thought that putting away my gender was the answer to that. After enough coaxing, I eventually bought into it myself.

"Maybe you're right, mom. You usually are." I dabbed an escaped tear with my sandpaper napkin.

In the days following Krissy's departure, I learned that seemingly everyone had known she was planning on breaking up with me except me. It's all over my medical records. Staff considered how I would handle it and debated how and when I should find out. By the time Krissy told me, I was the last to know. It was kind of her to wait until I got out of the ICU, but the whole thing was confusing and bothersome. Why did she pick the day she did? Why was she making this decision to break up so abruptly and so convincingly?

I shoveled another spoonful of ice cream into my mouth. There's never enough ice cream when I'm mourning, let alone inside a tiny

Styrofoam cup. I scraped the bottom as carefully as I scraped resin when I smoked crack. Every tiny bit mattered.

I had little else to enjoy. Things felt so oppressively dark.

There was one positive: the visit from the doctor who treated me while I was in the ICU. A shorter man with reddish brown hair and square-framed glasses, he came unannounced, bearing a Bible. Knowing I'd written a book, he brought excerpts of some things he'd written. He thought I might relate. In the Bible, he marked some passages he thought relevant to my journey and inscribed a message in the front.

"I honestly didn't think you would survive based on your condition," he said, as he slid the Bible across the table to me. "I see this as a miracle. The Lord intervened."

Stunned that a doctor would make such specific Christian statements at a county hospital, I accepted the gift and thanked him for helping save my life. I'm not sure if I meant the words or not.

During the day, I did my best to put on my happy face. But at night I carried my sadness to my room and buried myself in blankets to muffle the echo of my sobbing cries. On more than one night, I found myself looking around for tools to kill myself, but realized this hospital had done a damn good job of removing self-injurious items. So I settled on self-strangulation while hidden under my covers. What overnight tech would ever take care enough to actually look under the covers to see if I was breathing? This seemed foolproof. I tried to fight the urge, but the emotional pain became too much to take. One night I finally took a pillowcase and wrapped it around my neck tightly enough that it cut off my circulation. But as soon as I got myself into a position where I might've been able to get the job done, I became overwhelmed with the thought that I didn't want to die in a psychiatric ward. With the pressure in my head intensifying, I knew I was running out of time and frantically fought to untie the pillowcase I'd so meticulously knotted.

Like a diver out of oxygen, I raced with urgency to break through to the surface before finally taking in a gasping breath of air. Beads of sweat streamed down my forehead as I lay back on the bed with heavy breaths.

I was not going to end up a psych ward ghost story.

FOR ALL THE discussion among the professionals about the severity of my mental health problems, though, it wasn't helping that my gender was still pressing at the very fabric of my being. They knew gender dysphoria was at the heart of my current psychiatric crisis. Yet they were so inconsistent with their use of name and pronouns that a social worker actually wrote a note in my chart to advise the doctors, nurses, and various other personnel to please use male pronouns and the name Nate. The very next note was written by a nurse, referring to me as Jen, "she," and "her."

The more the various staff in the hospital referred to me as a female, the more I wanted to suppress my struggles. It seemed far easier than trying to correct people at every turn. If I could just convince myself to be Jen and act like a woman, things would be much easier.

Nate was just dying to come out, though. Krissy had written in her letter describing how she found me that she believed Jen died that morning of December 4, 2011, and Nate was born. It was one point we could still agree on. Under the irritating fluorescent lights of the visiting room with my mom, though, I was having a hard time putting Jen to rest. Not only because I saw the name on my hospital wristband and was referred to as "she" and "her" by most staff, but it also turned out a guy on a different floor of the psych ward was interested in me. As unhealthy as it sounds, I appreciated Jeff's tokens of affection, sent through notes and other creative means. And he was interested in me as a female.

It was just what I needed to take my mind off Krissy—and my gender.

I set the empty ice cream cup back on the food tray and pulled my feet up on the chair, spoon still in my mouth. All the gender stuff was too much to deal with, given everything else going on. The hospital staff's inconsistency was only making my identity feel more unstable than it already was, too. Maybe Mom was right. Maybe I needed to just put it aside.

I tossed the spoon to the tray, where it made a soft landing in the remnants of the applesauce. "What time do you leave tomorrow?"

"Flight's at 1:30. I don't know if I'll be able to make it back up here again before I go," she said. She was sitting with her thighs on her palms, kicking her feet up and down on the ground to soothe the restless leg syndrome that drives her to nightly misery. "I'm not moving too fast these days."

My mom's hair was greyer than I recalled it being the last time she'd come to Minneapolis. She seemed to have shrunk another inch as well. She'd had multiple hip replacements and a neck fusion, was facing ankle and foot surgery, and still had a back so bad she was at risk of paralysis. Her health had been a source of worry for me since I'd been her caregiver a decade earlier. She'd slowed down since then, but her legs were still crawling and kicking at high intensity. For all the adversity she'd been through, her being there to support me as I struggled with gender dysphoria following my suicide attempt was a testament to her love for me.

She didn't want to let go of Jen. She didn't want to lose her daughter. But she'd do anything for me as her child. She hopped a plane as soon as Krissy told her about the suicide attempt. For all intents and purposes, my mom knew it was happening before Krissy did. Krissy had walked out of the house the morning of the attempt and forgotten her keys. I proceeded to lock her out. After she left, she called her mom and then my mom.

My mom told her she needed to go back to the house. Motherly instinct told her I was not safe. Krissy didn't want to go back. Her own mom didn't want her to, either. But my mom implored her.

My mom recalls with vivid accuracy telling her, "I'm serious, Krissy. If ever there was a time that my child was going to take steps to end her life, it is right now. I am telling you, you need to return to that house immediately."

Reluctantly, Krissy did. "It's locked," she told my mom. "I don't have my keys."

Sensing the urgency of the situation with a sensitivity only a parent can possess, she ordered Krissy to immediately find a way into the house. Downstairs, I'd heard a knock at that time.

"There's no answer," Krissy told my mom flatly.

"Oh my God. Break a window then," she said. "Krissy, you have got to get in there right now!" She was practically begging Krissy to take action.

The reality of my mom's words finally sunk in. Krissy broke one of the garden-level windows and climbed inside the basement to find me unresponsive.

My mom's instinct had been right. Had Krissy listened to her own emotions—or her own mother—I would not have survived. It was only because of my mom's instructions that Krissy was willing to find a way into our house and subsequently save my life.

Things spiraled out of control soon after. Krissy and her mom were none too hospitable with my mom upon her arrival. They said very few words and behaved very secretively. Turns out, they were apartment hunting for Krissy.

THAT DAY IN the psych ward, as my mom and I sipped stale coffee that had been on the burner for twelve hours, we were both pissed off as we talked about how Krissy and her mom handled the situation. My mom was suddenly my closest support, my best friend, and my source of all information for what was happening at my house while I was locked up. And here we were also agreeing that although Nate existed, perhaps Jen deserved one more shot at life.

I got up from my chair and walked towards hers, kneeled down, and squeezed her in a hug. There was no place I'd rather have been than wrapped tightly in my mom's protective warm arms as thirty-one years of heartache and pain came pouring out. I was losing everything in my life all at once. I was in shock. Despite her reservations about my gender, she was the only person on Earth I could trust to not turn her back on me.

But like everyone else, she too had to leave.

"RISE AND SHINE! You've got treatment in fifteen minutes." Light broke through the open door until it closed again with a thud. A woman entered the dark room and set a pair of scrubs on my bed. "Put these on. No bra or underwear underneath, okay?"

As if I'd be wearing a bra.

I put my fancy beige rubber-soled socks on the cold tiled floor. What was I about to get myself into? Electroconvulsive therapy? Did I really agree to this?

All I could think about was the shock therapy depicted in *Girl, Interrupted* or *One Flew Over the Cuckoo's Nest*. ECT has been used for decades for a variety of reasons—some ethical, some not. People are often surprised to learn it's still used for treatment of mental illness, as it is typically seen to be an archaic treatment. Indeed I believe it is. Still, some providers swear by it. Others maintain it does nothing but create more problems. Some mental health workers will actually have their clients sign contracts stating they will not agree to ECT. Apparently, in my postcoma stupor and while lacking my full faculties to make informed decisions about my own health care, I agreed to the suggestion. I was at the end of my rope with my mental health. Meds had been causing so many problems for so long that everything I tried resulted in side effects that outweighed the benefit.

I was running out of options.

ECT was a last-ditch effort to try *something, anything* to help my mental health. More specifically, the treatment was designed to help treat what I'd first been diagnosed with at age twelve: severe depression. Yet that diagnosis was starting to seriously be questioned by the hospital psychiatrist, as well as my neurologist.

I switched out of my comfy sleeping attire for chlorine-scented turquoise scrubs that contained enough starch to stand up and walk on their own and with the letters HCMC emblazoned across my back. Like an inmate, I was now clearly identifiable as a psych ward patient.

The saggy pants and low-cut top did little to keep me covered, let alone warm. For as nervous as I should have been about the upcoming procedure, I was too lethargic and apathetic to care. I curled back under the covers to warm up until the technician arrived to escort me to the basement.

"Knock, knock. Ready to go?" The silhouette of a heavy-set man with jingly keys appeared in the room. I emerged from the cocoon of blankets I'd wrapped myself in and made my way to the door. "I've got a wheelchair for ya here, if you want it." His thick, hairy hands pushed the chair closer to me.

"I'm okay to walk. Thanks." I had no interest in looking any sicker than I already did. The depression, coma, and subsequent electrolyte battle had resulted in weight loss. I was thinner than I had been since I was strung out on crack. With my ghostly complexion, sunken cheeks, gaunt frame, and hunched posture, I looked sick enough—not to mention the still-bloodshot eyes and multihued bruising on my neck and face. And it didn't help that one of the IV sites on my arm had become infected and was hard and swollen at the crux of my elbow to the size of a ping-pong ball.

This inflammation of a vein, called phlebitis, was caused by prolonged IV use while I was comatose. The bruised lump on my left elbow only added to my sickly appearance. The scar from the IV still remains, inches from the scars where I'd cut myself before the suicide attempt, forever serving as visual reminders of the day my whole world changed.

I had searched my memory but could not recall ever signing up for ECT. But I had to let go of control and allow others to help me. After all, if they hadn't worked whatever "miracle" they had worked in the ER and ICU, I probably wouldn't be breathing. Whoever had recommended this must've thought I could really benefit from it.

"You sure you don't wanna lift?" the tech asked. "Free transport!" He smiled sheepishly, as if he was unsure if he should make jokes with a psych ward patient.

"Sure. Let's ride."

Fuck it. Who cared if I looked sick? I was in the hospital. That's where sick people go. I'd put on the tough front and abided by the "everything's fine" mantra Krissy had instilled in me for too long. I was recovering from a near-fatal injury. Who was going to judge me if I got a free ride to the basement? I had to remind myself that not only was it okay to accept help, especially in the hospital, but that I didn't need to put up the tough front anymore.

The tech escorted me and another patient through the double locked doors where Krissy had made her final exit. We wound around a maze of hallways to an out-of-the-way freight elevator.

This seemed fishy. "Where are you taking us? To a dungeon? That'd be appropriate for shock therapy, I suppose."

The tech laughed. The other patient, whose mental health and medications resulted in a stone-faced, blank stare, did not.

The door opened to a musty area surrounded by laundry bins, cleaning supplies, and old medical equipment. This didn't seem like the right area at all. Or maybe it was exactly where they wanted to hide their medical experiment dungeon, far out of sight from the others in the hospital. I looked around for a lobotomy chair, convinced that if I saw one, I was making a break for it, come hell or high water.

"You sure you know where you're going?" I asked, now questioning my rationale behind letting go and allowing others to help me.

"Yup. Just around this turn here." I half expected a mad scientist with a bloodied jacket, goggles, and static-charged white hair to emerge around the corner with a scalpel and maniacal laugh. Instead, the tech paused as we arrived. He pulled out a clipboard and jotted a few notes. "I'll be right back, and we'll get you a bed."

My compadre from the mental health unit began wandering off. *Not my problem*, I thought. What a relief to not have to take on others' problems for awhile. I had enough of my own.

THE DIMLY LIT room had a cold draft despite the number of workers scurrying about. To my right was the nurses' station, where young women in scrubs and white shoes dropped off papers and picked up others. All along the wall to my left was a line of beds, separated only by curtains. A chorus of beeps and buzzes blipped intermittently through the quiet voices of the staff and doctors.

The silence amid the sounds was oppressive. Something heavy was lurking in the air.

A curtain to one of the rooms was flung open with a high-pitched squeal. An older man in a white jacket and glasses emerged. His jacket was not bloodied, nor was he sporting goggles or wild hair. "All finished up in 6. Bring in the next patient," he said aloud to anyone within earshot. He stepped behind the nurses' station as the tech reapproached me.

"Alrighty, the nurses will take you from here. But so I can confirm I've transported the correct patient to the correct location, could you please confirm your name and date of birth?" A perplexed expression crossed his face as he looked at the chart to find my correct name.

I shook my head and looked down, once more shamed by my identity. I might as well just explain. "My legal name is Jennifer. They might have it noted that I go by Nate. I'm transgender. Or maybe I'm a freak."

Fumbling for a response, he hesitated, shifting his weight. "Oh. I see. Yes. I see both of those names here." His eyes darted around as he tried to form a polite response to a situation he'd likely never been confronted with. "Umm, let's make it easier then. What is your date of birth?"

I responded accordingly.

"Thank you, Ms. . . . er, uhh . . ."

"Mr.," I said.

"Thank you, Mr. Cannon." He bowed and nodded his head apologetically. I bowed my head from shame. The title Mr. didn't seem right. I was going to give Jen another chance at life. But the title Ms. felt completely wrong. There was no winning this battle. "I have one other patient here to get settled," the tech added. "Once you wake up from this procedure, I'll be back, and we'll head upstairs."

"Okeydoke. I'll just go with the flow."

Why was I so calm about this? I hadn't had any med changes. Were they slipping something in my water? More likely, the eighteen to twenty very large needle pokes of Botox I'd gotten every ten weeks for nearly three years had thickened my skin. Or perhaps I figured this would be a piece of cake compared to being in a coma. Or maybe, just maybe, I was looking forward to the drugs: the anesthesia, the sedation, and that rush of feeling that comes with losing consciousness. Not only is it a high, but when you're unconscious you can't feel, can't think, can't process how shitty your life has become.

A young blond woman in blue scrubs, distinctive from my turquoise inpatient scrubs, approached with a perky smile. "Well, good morning there." She looked down at my wristband with the same perplexed look the tech had given his clipboard. "Okay, so you're Jennifer?"

Here we go again. "I . . . yeah . . . technically speaking. I go by Nate because I'm a tranny. You can just call me 'It.'"

"Well, we won't do that. How would you like to be addressed?"

Much like Mr. versus Ms., I had to think about this. I was offended when people called me Jen, but Nate didn't feel right either. As my mom and I agreed before she departed, perhaps I had too much on my plate to tackle that part of my problems just yet.

I put my head in my hands and ran my fingers through my short hair as I sighed. "I don't know. I don't care anymore. I just want to get this done." The cold drafts in the room blew a shiver through my bones. Thankfully all my times in the hospital made me aware of one of the best perks they offer: heated blankets fresh from a microwave.

"Could I get a couple of those heated blankets? I'm freezing."

"Sure," she said, wheeling me past the blankets into a closet-sized space between two curtains. "I'll be right back." She closed the curtain behind her.

It was just me and a very peculiar room now. A room with a bed that had five-point restraints: one for the head, one for each arm, and one for each leg. On a metal tray next to the bed rested an array of tools. A reflex hammer and eye light were easily identifiable, as were the EKG and EEG machines. I'd had plenty of experience with those since I was misdiagnosed with epilepsy back in 2008. But what was this apparatus that looked like a pair of dentures? On the other side of the bed was an IV bag, a vitals monitor, and two paddles that resembled external defibrillator paddles used to shock someone's heart back into rhythm after cardiac arrest.

What had I signed myself up for?

I'd already had my fair share of heart, lung, and breathing complications. I wasn't looking forward to having these paddles applied to each side of my brain, to force me into a seizure. I'd had enough of those in my life, too. On the bright side, at least I'd be out cold, dreaming of a better life, while my brain was being barbecued. Who knows, maybe it would even kill me.

The curtain opened, and the young blond women returned. "Alright, two nice warm blankets for ya. What I'll have you do is lay down here on the bed on your back, okay? Then I'll get an IV started."

I crawled up on the bed, trying to ignore the restraints. It came out of me anyway. "Are you going to restrain me?"

"They would only be used as necessary for your safety. Don't worry—we don't put them on tight."

Mmm-hmm.

I watched as the nurse began preparing an IV. Another needle. She looked down at my left arm and saw the bandage. "Ooh, looks like we won't use that vein. We can use your right arm, though."

Sure. Why not?

She sterilized the area and inserted the needle before taping it down. She reached over to the IV machine and started the drip. "This is just saline, so you won't feel anything from it. Hang tight here, and I'll let the anesthesiologist know you're ready."

Whatever you say.

The woman stepped out as the light overhead shone directly down on me like a spotlight.

I lay on the bed and tried not to think of the movie depictions of what I was doing. None of this seemed real. This felt like *A Clockwork Orange*. For as scared as I was, it was almost a deer-in-the-headlights response. Even though I questioned whether I wanted to go through with a highly controversial medical therapy, I was also at a point where I was willing to try anything, to go along with anything. After all, if I just let things happen and didn't fight or react, I'd be able to get out of the hospital sooner.

Then I could get on with my suicide that had been so rudely interrupted.

Despite losing some heat, the blankets added to my increasingly heavy grogginess. I pulled the covers up under my chin and rolled to my side. As I did, the room seemed to spin. Whatever was in the bag must've had something more than just saline.

Space and time vanished before a male voice brought me to attention. "Good morning!" it said. The dim light peering down at me from the ceiling sparked to fluorescent white as he flipped a switch on the wall behind the hospital bed.

"Nice to meet you," the man said, holding out a hand. I retrieved my hand from under the blanket and reciprocated his greeting. "I'm Dr. Duggen, the anesthesiologist. I have a couple questions. Have you ever had any sort of reaction to anesthesia?"

How was I to know how I handled the anesthesia while comatose? What a stupid thing to ask. "Uhh, well, I can't speak to when I was in a coma. Before I got my dystonia diagnosis, I had a facet joint injection.

Either my heart rate or blood pressure dropped. It wasn't enough to be dangerous, but they made me aware of that. Then I puked. And felt awful for a few days."

What the fuck was in this IV drip? What an inopportune time to pose questions about my medical history. Had they asked for my consent to participate in ECT while I was this groggy, too? I closed my eyes as the objects around me started to spin.

"Do you remember what drug they used?"

"No."

He stepped around the bed to access the IV bag. "Okay, well, we'll go ahead and proceed with standard anesthesia then. I'm going to give you something now to help you relax."

"Is it Versed?" I asked. "I got really loopy from Versed when I first dislocated my shoulder and they put it back in its socket in the ER."

"Yup. We'll start with Versed. It'll make you a little sleepy. Go ahead and close your eyes if you'd like."

Before I knew it, the drug hit. Unlike when I was fifteen and had dislocated my shoulder, I did not explode into laughter. But I was dancing on a pillow top of fluffy cumulus clouds and sunshine; my brain began to smile. It'd been a long time since I had that sort of high. As soon as it came, it vanished.

"This is a little oxygen now," a voice said. "Just breathe normally."

I looked up with fun-house vision to see a gas mask lowering to my face. Initially, such masks always seem suffocating. I fought the stickiness of the airflow to draw in a deep breath.

"Good, now exhale," a voice grew deeper and calmer, "Inhale. And . . . exhale." The rhythm grew hypnotic.

THE DIM LIGHT was back again.

I sat up to see I was alone, on a bed, sticky pads stuck to my chest. My jaw throbbed, radiating pain through my gums. The pounding of my head grew so intense, I half expected to feel nails sticking out of the sides of my head like the screws in Frankenstein's monster's neck.

The pressure squeezed my eyes to a forced squint. The lights were too bright. The room was still spinning, making each wave of nausea crash harder against the harbor of my empty stomach.

A woman in blue scrubs and the man in the white coat returned, alerted to my consciousness by my change in vitals.

"How are you feeling?"

"Shitty," I said, putting my head in my hands. "My head and jaw are killing me. And I feel like I'm gonna puke." I laid my head back on the pillow, but the spins only worsened. I sat back up once more, expecting to heave.

"We'll do a cognitive assessment on you when you get back upstairs. For now we just want to make sure you stay stable here for a little while." The nurse switched out the IV bag.

"Why? Or, wait, what? Where am I? The ER?"

"No. You just completed ECT therapy. You just came out of sedation. Dr. Duggen would like to speak with you about how it went."

I braced myself.

7

Discharged

The doc returned, accompanied by the nurse. They'd been checking my ICU records. "You had a similar issue while under anesthesia there. It appears you have a long QT interval." He proceeded to describe a cardiac condition I'd never heard of, but that involves an abnormal electrical discharge causing an elongation between two waves of the heartbeat. He explained he wouldn't give me Zofran, a common anti-nausea med given during anesthesia, to avoid complications.

"It shouldn't impact ECT therapy. However, you may want to see a cardiologist to get it checked out. It may be nothing, but it can also be a very serious condition."

Once again informed of medically relevant details at a cognitively inopportune time, I implored myself to grasp and cling to the words despite the haze still wafting through my freshly sizzled brain. I'd just barely woken up from the anesthesia that was fucking with my heartbeat, after having my brain fucked with by a machine that was literally frying it. Just a week or two after being comatose in a hypothermic state. There are better times to tell someone they have a heart condition.

The conversation made its impression, though. The idea of now having an electrical abnormality with my heartbeat was almost comforting. Maybe, I hoped, I'd finally just drop dead while running or something.

I don't recall going back to the ward. ECT splotched the memories of much of the rest of the hospital stay. What recollections I do have are more of people and places, rooms and repeated events—most of which blur together. In the hospital, every day is exactly the same. The coupling of my shock treatments with the droning redundancy of psych ward life led my brain to retain only snapshot images, highly filtered and hazy. But certain aspects remain blazingly bright in my memory, namely the groggy nausea after every shock treatment. I struggled to eat. What I did eat tasted burnt, coppery, like chewing on pennies. I couldn't think clearly; my circuitry felt electric and my brain fried, far more than any street drug or alcoholic drink ever left it feeling.

AFTER ONE OF the many treatments, I returned to the ward to shower, feeling shaky and uneasy about my sureness for standing. After muscling my way through the solo process, a right I'd had to earn back, I stood under the stream, chin to my chest, wishing the water could cleanse my life circumstances.

I donned my special socks and scrubs and headed to the dining area to try to force down breakfast. I was never hungry following ECT, quite the opposite, but breakfast is by far the most important (and in my opinion the best) meal of the day. I'm used to getting up and putting a bowl of oatmeal in the microwave before my eyes are even fully open. But ECT necessitated that I fast. Being unable to eat for twelve hours is a big challenge for my body.

I pulled my tray from the cart, the last one left. Cold pancakes and room-temperature milk for a tiny box of cereal awaited me, along with a delectable assortment of fruit. I soaked the pancakes in extra syrup and pressed my plastic spork into the dough, tiny bubbles of sugary goodness oozing from the golden-brown edges. A woman approached the table, interrupting my pancake experience.

"Jennifer, you can finish your breakfast later, but the doctor's ahead of schedule and ready for you now."

"*Now?* I just sat down! The appointment isn't for twenty minutes."

You gotta savor every moment of happiness you can when you're locked in a psych ward for weeks. Despite being cold and rubbery, I wanted those damn pancakes. And being hungry to the point I felt weak made me very irritable.

I had a few choice words for the nurse for calling me Jennifer. Assertive, perhaps slightly aggressive, but ultimately logical and fact based. I finished up my cakes, shoved my tray in the cart, and headed to the doctor's room.

This wasn't what I had planned. I was going to use the time I was savoring my syrup-soaked hockey pucks to figure out questions, plan my course for the appointment. Though I'd been seeing this psychiatrist for a couple weeks, only recently had the shock treatment and the medication had a chance to start working.

The duration of ECT treatment necessitated a longer in-patient stay. That, in turn, gave my team more time to sort out my mood symptoms. That morning we would discuss what my psychiatrist and my neurologist were working together to figure out. Did I actually have bipolar disorder? Had I been living with the wrong diagnosis for almost twenty years?

I entered the room. Dr. Myers and his wife, also a psychiatrist, sat waiting. He picked his head up from jotting notes on his computer.

"Well, good morning," he said. "How was the ECT?"

I'd lost faith in psychiatry long ago, but Dr. Myers was giving me hope. He'd been quite kind in allowing me privileges not usually afforded to patients. Most notably, he allowed me to go out running. On the days I didn't have ECT, I'd rise early, far too early to do anything productive on a psych unit. But I was on a schedule with my sleep and had come to love getting up early in the morning. It's when I feel most alive. It's also when my dystonia is easiest to work with.

Most of the time, I'd head to the small kitchenette area and make myself a packet of plain oatmeal. No sugar or syrup or fruit was available to top it with, and each day it seemed to taste more like Styrofoam. I'd mill around, stretch, and wait. They wouldn't let me run until 8 a.m. I certainly couldn't have my shoes, since they had laces, so I'd sit by the nurses' station and as soon as the clock allowed, request my shoes. They'd hand them over, I'd lace them up, and they'd let me free. For one hour.

For some reason, despite being close enough to run to my own house, or a bar, or in front of a train, I didn't. I got in my miles, enjoyed my high, and returned to the ward on time. As was expected.

Dr. Myers appreciated that I was respectful of the time he allowed me and didn't abuse it. So, too, he understood just how crucial exercise, particularly running, was to my mental health. He and his wife were both runners themselves.

"I'm sure they mentioned the heart thing? The long QT?" I asked him. He had no response. "All I know is I feel fuzzy in my brain. I can't think straight, and my head hurts all the time. So does my jaw."

He leaned back, brow slightly furrowed, clearly immersed in intense thought.

"Well, as we discussed when you agreed to the treatment, we decided to do both hemispheres. Doing the left hemisphere can lead to an increased risk of memory issues, and we know from your EEGs that you already have abnormalities in the left side of your brain."

I didn't recall agreeing to having both hemispheres fried. I didn't recall agreeing to ECT at all. At my request, he pulled a form from his file. It had my signature on it. I'd agreed to it. Perhaps I felt pressured to buy in and give the docs what they wanted. Or perhaps I signed simply because I'd been signing so much crap that I could no longer read fine print.

Dr. Myers's explanation concerned me. "Why would you do the left side if you knew I had left hemisphere abnormalities on the EEG?"

He explained it was more successful in helping severe mental health symptoms, especially those recalcitrant to medication.

"The Lamictal may help settle some of those brain wave abnormalities, but I still feel that doing both hemispheres is the best route for your case. How is the medication going, by the way?" I'd been on the lowest dose possible for almost two weeks. They were going slow with me. "Any side effects you're noticing?"

I didn't know. Maybe? The effect of the ECT treatment convoluted any sort of clear sense regarding the oral medication I'd started. So far it didn't seem to be having any serious side effects, unlike how I'd felt on other meds, and that was amazing. Not wanting to ruin a potentially good thing, I pinned the headache, brain fog, and everything else on ECT.

"Usually on anti-depressants, I start getting night sweats about two weeks in. That hasn't happened yet," I said.

"Well, that's a good sign!" Dr. Myers's wife chimed in. A blond woman with an appearance that could rival that of any starlet on a magazine cover, she and her husband worked as a team. I appreciated people willing to work diligently with my neurology team to help me. But I wasn't prepared for a picturesque couple who shared a passion for running races, helping patients, and still maintaining what appeared to be a happy marriage of over twenty years.

How sickeningly successful. I'd just lost my relationship after losing my career and many of the activities I enjoyed doing with my own partner, and now I had a happy husband-wife team as my psychiatrists? To this day it seems odd, and, in retrospect, I think I trusted them too much.

"Yeah, I guess this is going quite well compared to other meds," I said. I meant what I said. It was going better than many other meds, but the performer in my brain knew it was time to go on stage. This meeting would influence how much longer I'd have to stay in the hospital. I didn't want to do anything that would keep me locked up any longer than necessary. So there would be no complaints about meds. No fussing about ECT. I'd raised my concerns; now it was time to look happy and act calm, cool, collected.

"How is the depression?" Dr. Myers asked. They didn't need to know about the pillowcase incident. They didn't need to hear that I was still having incessant, nagging suicidal thoughts. I just needed to stick to the script and fake it until I could make it to discharge. I'd figure out what to do after that, but getting out had to be my primary goal.

"It's okay," I said. "Some negative thinking, thinking I blew my relationship, screwed up everything again. But I truly believe everything happens for a reason, and I believe there's a reason I'm still alive. More and more, I want to live and be well. I'm tired of being sick."

They bought it, perhaps reluctantly so. I tried, so hard, to buy it myself and believe in my own words. They knew that I knew exactly what to say—and what not to say. But they didn't fight me on it or press for more details.

Dr. Myers opened his laptop, which he'd closed upon my entrance.

"I'm glad to hear things are going well. We'll up your dose of the Lamictal and see how you do. If we keep on with that and ECT, I'd expect you'd be able to be discharged by Christmas."

That date was fast approaching.

He cleared his throat and pushed the laptop forward on the rectangular white table, the long fluorescent lights glaring down on it so sharply it shimmered.

I sat up in my chair, identical to the ones in the patient lounge area. My dystonia was truly beginning to hate chairs. They were everywhere, too.

The couple exchanged glances, coded language between them developed through two decades of marriage. I'd had that similar ability with Krissy: we could look at each other and tell what the other was thinking. But I couldn't tell what these two were thinking.

The woman took the lead.

"So we'd like to talk to you about your diagnosis," she said. "We've had a number of discussions with you, read the charting and background medical info, and even got a chance to read your book." She pulled a stack of papers from her briefcase. "It's very good, by the way. Thank you for sharing it with us."

"Sure," I said. "I hope it's helpful."

"It was." Dr. Myers straightened his tie, while his wife filed through a stack of papers to retrieve a note. She slid it across the table to him.

"I've also had a chance to talk to your neurologist, as you know. He agrees Lamictal would be a good choice for you and concurs that your mental health symptoms could be helped by it." He went on to explain the mechanism of Lamictal and how it functions. It helps stabilize brain waves thought to be involved in mood instability. He also noted that SSRIs, the most common class of anti-depressants, are known to worsen manic symptoms in patients with bipolar. Perhaps that was why I seemed to have such adverse reactions to them.

"I still can't rule out bipolar II, but I'd like you to follow up with mental health."

Bipolar II is different from bipolar I in that in bipolar I you have either outright psychosis or hallucinations or delusions. In bipolar II, you experience hypomania, a less extreme form of that same energy that pushes the brain over the edge into mania.

I'd never had a psychotic episode. I'd not been one to hallucinate or have delusions outside of my crack addiction days, either. So by default, that would bring a bipolar II diagnosis. My sister had been diagnosed with bipolar II about five years earlier. There seems to be a familial aspect to the illness.

The diagnosis officially stayed as major depression. But now it read: "with a differential of bipolar II (chronic)." Why chronic was stipulated I don't know. But it seemed to make sense. I was chronically thinking about suicide. Chronically mired in the mess of my own brain, convinced I was a failure. Chronically wishing my life had been different, that I'd done things differently.

I was sick of feeling that way. Bipolar had been suspected since I was in college. Something else always got blamed for my symptoms. The drugs. The alcohol. The brain injuries. The ADHD. The anxiety. For the first time, doctors seemed to be leaning towards it with certainty, but still they wouldn't change my diagnosis entirely.

I don't fit the profile for major depression, and I haven't since I was twelve. But they still weren't convinced enough to outright change it to bipolar II. After reading the symptoms for myself, they seemed a better fit than the diagnosis I'd been living with for nearly twenty years.

I understood the doctor's direction to follow up with psychiatry about medication as well as diagnosis upon discharge. I'd have to keep up with some form of mental health treatment anyway if I ever wanted to transition. But I'd probably have more of a need for that treatment if I did *not* transition.

The psychiatrists agreed.

I LEFT THE meeting feeling optimistic. Maybe we were on to something with the Lamictal. It was at least a step in the right direction. I called my mom, who already knew about my possible diagnosis of bipolar II. She seemed to agree that fit better than a depression diagnosis but wanted to talk about travel arrangements. She was practically imploring me to come stay with her in North Carolina for awhile after I was discharged.

My family has deep roots in North Carolina. My paternal great-great-grandfather started Cannon Mills in Kannapolis. The city remained unincorporated, and the Cannon family became well known for both their generosity and their paternalistic control, giving back to the community where the workers lived, even as the mills became the largest and most powerful in the world. For decades, the family ran pretty much everything in town, including the police.

In the early '80s, the company sold the mills. Textile manufacturing had moved overseas, and the Cannon brand had lost its standing in the market. But the brand was sold. My family name was sold.

I remain branded by the family's wealth and the fact that my father, who still lives in North Carolina, has been unwilling to be a part of my life. When my mom moved to North Carolina from Iowa, it became very difficult to figure out how to visit her for reasons far beyond geography.

I twirled my fingers around the phone cord, elbows propped up on the small table separating the two patient phone stations on the ward.

"I just don't want you going back into that house after all this." My mom's voice shook not with tremors but from beating her feet against the ground to offset her restless leg syndrome. I could hear the strain in her voice. Her precarious health always wore heavily on my mind.

I didn't have any pressing need to be in Minneapolis itself for awhile. I needed to find a place to live. But to do that, I needed a job. Yet I was waiting on a Social Security verdict, so I couldn't search for a job until I knew what it was. There was no winning. I'd have to stay in the house until things got figured out.

Surely there was no rush.

"Alright mom, fine. I'll come."

An abrupt question followed. "How long can you stay?" She'd want me to stay forever, but eventually I'd have to return to the realm of the normal. I'd been away from my usual life and routine for weeks. I missed Ferrick, my sweet black cat with the white triangle on his chest. He had to be getting confused by my absence.

Before I could list any more reasons, it was settled. I flew to the not-so-trans-friendly state of North Carolina. What joy. While there, though, all I could think about was Minneapolis. Something told me I was supposed to be there. I was missing something important.

My irritability grew greater each day and became visible to my mom and her husband. They called me Jen. I didn't know if I wanted that or not. I didn't know if I should expect them to call me Nate. People who heard about my suicide attempt came out of the depths of the interwebs to contact me and wish me well. Each one addressed me as Jennifer.

I tried my best to play along and embrace the role. I appreciated their condolences and encouragement. But how was I to manage that if I was still wrestling with something too painful to disclose? Much like the congratulations after the book launch, the messages didn't sit right with me. Seeing my female name felt disturbingly wrong.

The urge to flee my body, ever-present, grew more pressing. I wanted to run away—as far and as fast as possible. But the back woods of North Carolina are no place for a person of questionable gender. I knew I wasn't welcome in those parts. I certainly couldn't move forward with gender reassignment while there.

If that's what I wanted, that is. My mom made convincing arguments as to why I should wait each time I brought it up. Jeff, my bipolar beau, was out of the hospital. "He really seems to like you," she'd say. "I think you should give it a shot."

She meant it with such a good heart. She really did just want things to be normal for me for once. That's all she ever wanted. If I could just be a woman and find that right guy, maybe things would start to work out. I believed her. I got to know him, kept up the gender performance, put on the show. But I knew in my heart my gender would resurface, try as I might to shove it back into a closet.

8

Heartless

I returned from the visit to my mom's, tracking one lonely set of January footprints through the crunchy Minnesota snow as I walked from the bus stop to the house I'd told others for years was going to kill me. Feeling a stranger in the home I'd owned for over five years, I hesitated as I put the key in the door. Inside, the air felt stagnant, almost dead. Something was different. But the kitchen I walked into was the same.

It was the room that sold us on the house. We loved the bay window with the creeping vines, the spacious airiness, the beautiful cabinetry. This time the space felt different, though—hollow, empty. A gushing wound of memories spewed out faster than I could keep up, flooding my consciousness. The fights, the fun, the love. But now it was just me and Ferrick. Just me, him, and the damn house I had been trying so hard to get out of.

I dropped my backpack on a chair at the kitchen table. In doing so I got a glimpse of the living room. Krissy's glass-covered coffee table—which she had made herself out of hockey sticks she collected while playing in college—was gone. That item meant more to her than just about anything she owned. Next would be the rubber tree, which typically sat in the corner of the living room next to the front-facing window. It, too, was gone.

Throughout the house, items of hers were gone. Her closet was empty, as were the drawers of her dresser. Her wall art no longer decorated the halls, and her desk was absent from the corner of the low-ceilinged attic bedroom that doubled as a spare room and her office. The guest bed that had been in there was also missing.

Everything important to her was gone. And most importantly, so was she.

THE WEIGHTED EMPTINESS in the air left me nearly lightheaded. I took a seat on the ratty, old two-seat couch with broken springs she left in our upstairs TV room.

Memories of our relationship flashed through my head. I'd told my mom for years that I wasn't happy in the relationship, that Krissy was changing. I'd told Krissy she would be better off without me. I was only holding her back from doing things she wanted to do. My limitations did indeed come between us. So, too, did my gender identity. The pain of the moment—and of the realization of the reasons why the sound in the house suddenly went hollow—weighed on my shoulders.

We had had something special. But without being able to get gay married, we couldn't get gay divorced. And since she was the corporate bigwig making six figures and nearing completion of her MBA, it made sense that she had control over our finances. But she was done being nice.

I picked up my cell and called my mom.

"Mom," I said, pinching back emotion. "She's gone. She's not here. There's nothing here. There's nothing here but Ferrick. She's gone. Everything's gone . . ." I trailed off as unexpectedly urgent emotion hit me. I started weeping, unable to speak complete sentences through my sobs. It wouldn't have mattered in the conversation anyway. The house was built like a fortress, and since Krissy had the cable, internet, and phone disconnected, my mom caught only every third word.

"I'm sorry, sweetie. I'm having a . . ." Her words cut in and out.

I hung up as frustrated as I had been before I picked up the phone. It was a cell on Krissy's plan, with the cell phone company she worked for. It was only a matter of time until I lost that, too. I threw the phone down on the carpet half hoping it would shatter and die. It managed to survive. Just as I had.

How could she have moved out so quickly, without me or my mom knowing?

I knew Krissy's mom had been in town while I was in the hospital. My mom told me that. But what we didn't know was that the two of them had found her an apartment. She took only what was most important to her and left the rest.

I don't care about things. Possessions and money can't hold you at night. They can't give or receive love. They can't eat meals or have conversations with you. Yet they are the foundation for the memories that make a home.

Energy emanating from the items once so key to the life we'd built seemed to swallow the air. The ghosts of both my former life partner and my former self haunted every step.

AIR TRAFFIC RUSH hour started at 7 p.m. as usual. The anger and self-loathing were amplified as the planes rumbled overhead, drilling sound-based memories into my already cluttered head. Jeff, my burglar boyfriend, came over to chill. Charming and cute with his newspaper boy hat, he had wooed me in whatever way he could while we were on different floors of the hospital. He continued those efforts after he got out. But I received his advances primarily out of revenge. The relationship was a very bad fit for me. He was interested in me as a woman despite knowing I went by Nate. In retrospect, I don't think he understood it. Nevertheless, he filled my need for companionship, and the idea of having someone other than Krissy interested in me was very appealing.

Just two weeks after losing a ten-year relationship, I had a boyfriend. And with my mom's encouragement, I was going to do my damnedest to be Jen. I needed to find a way to make it work. I grasped and clung to any aspect of my femaleness that I could.

Just look where being trans had gotten me so far.

I HAD TO start somewhere. First step: peel myself off the ground and start again. Piece by piece, I tried to reassemble a life. But before I could do that, I needed to reclaim my independence. I broke it off with newspaper boy as it became clear that he was merely looking for a free pad to crash at, and it didn't feel right to have him at the house Krissy had agreed to pay the mortgage on for four months. Besides, I needed to get through this time alone, independently.

Krissy had imposed via email a stern deadline on me: she expected me out of the house and for it to be sold by the end of April. It wasn't that far off. Weeks passed, and the February snow was starting to melt, causing the ice dam over the back door to start seeping water down the window frames. Just as in years past, I spent quality time with Ziploc baggies, taping and retaping them to the window to catch the water as it fell. It was something Krissy had never been willing to deal with.

It reminded me of the wasp nest I'd warned her about that she sprayed with Raid. It didn't help. It took having ten wasps inside the house every day before she was willing to hire an exterminator. And the pipes that were clearly in need of more than just the Drano she poured down them had to nearly rust shut and start dripping in our basement before she was willing to call in a plumber. She put a Band-Aid on everything and ignored the underlying problem. The Band-Aids she'd tried to heal me with were peeling off, and it seemed she was no longer willing to deal with me and all of the problems inside my mind and body.

She wasn't going to be paying or contributing to the mortgage beyond April, period. After that, she would not put a penny towards the house, despite taking 100 percent of our savings. As if one can predict how long it will take to sell a home. And since she wasn't living there, she didn't have to pay the various bills, help prepare it for show, or be the one to keep it in show condition. She wouldn't have to tape baggies to the windows to hide an ice dam. She wouldn't have to arrange inspections or be responsible for the steps necessary just to get a house on the market in the first place.

That burden would fall all on me.

The pressure grew greater as she insisted I sign a listing agreement for the house. But with no money and no job, signing an agreement could have left me homeless. I'd received my Social Security Disability verdict, and just as I feared, my case had been denied. I had no choice but to get back into the workforce.

I delayed responding to Krissy and refused to sign, furiously applying for work. Finally, after a hundred applications, I got a hit. I was offered a part-time position as a concierge at Gables, an assisted living facility. The job itself was rewarding, I could physically do it, and management seemed to like me. But I wasn't going to be able to make ends meet on the low pay.

I didn't tell anyone there about my transgender limbo. I interviewed while presenting as female and didn't let them in on the secret. After all, I was going to put this gender dysphoria crap back in the closet for good.

I worked my position, and I kept applying for full-time gigs. I was willing to take anything, and in the end I got a customer service position doing scheduling for physical, occupational, and speech language therapy for persons with complex health care cases. The organization is well known in the Twin Cities as a resource center for people with brain and spinal cord injuries. I erroneously believed that management would be just as welcoming of me as they would of the many persons with visible disabilities they hire. Unfortunately, that was not the case. It was more than my dystonia could tolerate, and it forced me to reach out for accommodations. The process, however, would turn out to be an unparalleled exercise in frustration.

It was equally frustrating with insurance. Krissy had kept me on her insurance policy, with the threat pending that she was going to drop me at any time. I begged and pleaded with her to wait until I had employer-based insurance up and running. Even though our communication was done via email, the tension between us was increasingly thick. And with two jobs, I could no longer put off signing the listing agreement. As May brought unprecedented rain showers, I signed a name that no longer felt like mine to the dotted lines.

Finally, the house of cards hit the market.

MY MAIN GOAL at the time was to keep from killing myself long enough to get out of the house in the first place. Prepping a house for show while working sixty hours a week is not easy for anyone, let alone someone with my combination of conditions and circumstances. The gravity of it all was stooping my already hunched posture. The suicidal thoughts grew greater by the day.

It had been just four months since the attempt that caused Krissy to leave. I was starting to get serious about getting this suicide thing right. I just couldn't fight the urge anymore—the constant, incessant barrage of thoughts. I knew I had to do it when I had no obligations and when nobody would find me. That's easy when you live alone: nobody is around to check up on you, and the county sends you out the hospital doors without any sort of safety net in place.

I set it up almost like a shrine in the corner of the basement. There were the beach towels from Costa Rica and Florida on the treadmill belt. The posters of me that were used at my book launch, commemorating my first marathon and my first book. The stuffed animals we randomly acquired. A few key pictures from our past and all the legal documentation needed for identification.

Then there was the note. The CD, too, lest we forget the music. Words and music were my heart and soul for much of my life, and I wanted to recognize that in my death as well. I had written it all out, in various forms, for almost seven years. It changed shape to suit the times, the circumstances. But it was the same suicide note I'd been honing and crafting for years on end.

I was meticulous about it.

On the hand rail of the treadmill was a tie. It was knotted tightly. Wrapped around that knot was a bungee cord, to hold the knot in place and minimize any slipping that might occur when my body inevitably started to thrash.

A Cannon towel was ready for me to drape over my head: a symbolic closing to my own family's soap opera.

It was set.

I made a video on my computer explaining this was my suicide, not foul play. I then put on a CD of the songs I requested be played at my private service and approached the treadmill. I wrapped the tie around my neck and tied a knot. It was positioned to cut off airflow with minimal discomfort to my neck. I put the towel over my head as the pressure grew greater. I leaned forward and let the weight of my body fall on my neck, pressed firmly against the tie.

Images of my mom, niece, brother, Krissy, and others flashed through my mind as the pressure built and forced hallucinogenic sparks of colors. I could see my mom in mourning and feel her pain.

I thought of my own pain. The promise I'd made to myself. I'd vowed not to die in that house. I had made a promise to myself in the hospital that I would at least wait to kill myself until I could get out of that place. The urgency of the moment struck me. If I died there, I'd not only be dying in the house. I'd be dying as Jennifer Cannon.

I would have let my gender dysphoria kill me. I'd become another transgender suicide statistic. Another mentally ill suicide casualty. I'd be alienating Ferrick, who was counting on me to show him something was still stable in his life. I'd be hurting my family and what few friends I had remaining.

I'd have lost the fight.

My thoughts spun as I realized I had mere seconds to decide whether to live or die. This was going exactly where I wanted it to go. I was going to die. But I did not want to go into the light while still being Jennifer. That's just not who I was anymore, and it never would be, no matter how hard I tried. The internal dialogue continued as my vision weaved in and out of red and black overtones.

The discomfort maximized as my brain hit the crossroads of life and death. It was time to decide if I wanted to live or forever go to sleep.

My indecision forced my brain into action for me.

I reached up and removed the towel from my head before sliding two fingers just under the edge of the very taut ligature. It wasn't much, but it was enough. The kaleidoscope of colors slowed down, replaced by a fuzzy black film draping over my vision. I gasped for air and drew in a small breath. With my other hand I worked on untying the knot at the back of my neck. Frenzied but controlled tenacity drove me to dig deeper under the tie to get a little more air as my energy dwindled and my fingertips grew stiffer from the loss of blood flow. Finally, the knot broke free.

I ripped the tie from my neck and held it in my hands in front of me, crouched on the treadmill that seemed to be the center point of my suicide mission. I panted, chasing down my lost breath, as if in a full-on sprint. The pain of my ongoing problems with dystonia had been increasingly affecting my ability to run. In fact, it was stopping me in my tracks. What was the point of living anymore if I couldn't participate in activities that gave me meaning and purpose? Or if I was forced to run through life without being able to become who I really am?

I held my head in my hands until the floodgates broke loose and tears flowed as steadily as the spring rains. The silence of the old house magnified as I sat sniffling, reflecting, contemplating, questioning. What was happening to me?

I reflected on all my losses, including the increasing impact of dystonia on my running.

THE FIRST TIME it'd happened I thought it was a fluke. The ice was still melting. Maybe I'd just tripped over a chunk of ice or something. But then it happened again a few weeks later in the exact same way, and there was no ice, no cracks in the pavement, no unexpected curbs to blame it on.

I had long pants on the first time I fell. They absorbed the blow, but the impact still ripped a hole in my right knee. I was wearing shorts for the second one, and that same right knee bore the brunt of it.

Cruising along, I was in my runner's mind. The snow had melted to small dirty patches of ice on low-lying grassy areas, while life began to teem around me, filling my breaths with the refreshing lilac-scented beauty of spring. I lost myself in the pleasure of the moment and tried not to think about suicide.

The next thing I knew, I was on the ground. It happened so fast I had no time to brace myself. Thankfully I didn't have my right arm extended, which could have dislocated my shoulder. I put my hands down to lift myself up when my knee began to throb. I pushed myself up to my feet and looked down to see blood running down the front of my right leg. I had road rash and some pretty deep gouges. I didn't have any choice, though, but to press on. After a while the pain settled down, and I returned home with a bloody leg, a bloody sock, and a sense of bewilderment.

I SNAPPED BACK from the reminiscing and stared down from my position on the treadmill at my still healing knee. It had to have been an accident. Maybe it was my shoes or something. Or maybe this was a sign I had damaged my brain even more than it already had been in the suicide attempt less than six months earlier. Or maybe this was the progression of my dystonia. Either way, it felt hopeless.

I'd said for years that as long as my symptoms stayed above my waist, I'd be okay. I'd manage. But if dystonia interfered with my ability to run, it might as well strike me dead. Running gives me a natural high and a chemical and hormonal boost. It's a painkiller, wearing out my overactive muscles. I'd already lost hockey. Why was this passion also being taken from me?

I threw the tie down on the treadmill that symbolized so much. As much as I wanted to, I couldn't give into the suicidal urge yet. Despite the struggles, the emotional pain, the physical pain, the anger and regret, all of the loss, the mourning, the entire situation with Krissy leaving, being stuck in the house and forced to continue to work my tail off just to move forward with my gender when my neurological condition—I knew—was spreading to my right leg: despite all that, I *had* to get up and keep moving forward.

I knew I couldn't mention this close call with suicide to anyone. And I couldn't risk being told I could no longer run by telling anybody about my falls. Nor could I risk being told the ongoing progression of my neurological illness would make me ineligible for chest surgery or hormone therapy.

I certainly wouldn't mention to anyone how I'd started feeling my heart skip weirdly while running. That, too, started after the suicide attempt and was just another health-related issue I'd have to ignore if I wanted to be allowed to transition. I'd have to forge happiness if I wanted the gatekeepers' approval.

The Long QT syndrome put me at high risk for complications during surgery and in the rest of my life. Like the biomarkers in my bloodstream indicative of cardiac arrest, the Long QT interval arose after my suicide attempt. It was never there before, and I'd had plenty of heart tests. The condition can lead to dangerous arrhythmias and sudden death. This is most common during aggressive exertion, particularly swimming and running.

My worst nightmare was coming true. I'd lost the love of my life. My passion was being taken away. My neuro condition was spreading, and it seemed I'd damaged my heart when I failed to kill myself, too. And despite every ounce of me believing that it is imperative to find work that feeds the soul, I was working a full-time job I hated. It was horrible. But I had to see it as a temporary thing. I had to believe that if I became Nate—*truly* became Nate—and embraced it, perhaps I'd still have a shot at a happy life, dystonia, mental health challenges, and all.

Or maybe the Long QT would drop me dead while I was running. I would've been perfectly fine with that, too. I'd die doing what I love most.

I GOT UP from the treadmill and stood next to it, staring at the shrine I'd made to my own death.

"You can't kill yourself until you're out of this house and become a man," I said aloud. "You swore you wouldn't let this house or your gender kill you. It's gonna kill you, right here and now. This is what it wants. It wants you to kill yourself. Don't give it what it wants!" I turned and began pacing with rapidity to match that of my racing mind and heart. I kept thinking that I could not die as Jennifer in that house. That I could not die in that house—period. And I would not die as Jennifer—period. Both situations would require me to not only live and survive but to thrive and function: even if that meant working sixty-hour weeks with multiple jobs.

I vowed to myself at that moment that I would transition no matter what it cost me and that I would not allow my wish for death to result in suicide until I'd accomplished my mission of both getting out of that oppressive house and finding a home within my own skin.

Just like with addiction, I began to reframe my outlook on suicide: I didn't have to choose to never kill myself. I just had to choose to live for that day. One day at a time, one hour at a time, one minute at a time.

So it went. I worked despite the pain, ran despite the falls, and returned home daily to the house that was no longer my own but that I was responsible for. The spring rains had finally overpowered the clogged gutters and poured down the side of the house to soak the basement carpet, just days after the house went on the market. I sent pictures to Krissy, but she didn't want to pay to have it addressed.

I tried in vain to catch the rain. I'd put on my raincoat, drag out the big cooler, and head out to the side of the house, where I'd let it fill with water rushing from the gutters I couldn't reach to clean out. Then I'd haul it out to the street to dump it and return to do it all over again. Trip after trip, night after rainy night, I tried to minimize the damage being done to the house—already underwater in terms of the mortgage.

After much debate, she agreed to pay for the carpet to be cleaned in the basement. Thankfully I'd moved most of my boxes to a different area of the basement and avoided the water damage, but I'd have to move them for the cleaning anyway. Boxes of books do not, according to real estate agents, make for a showable house.

A few weeks later the gutters flooded the basement again. Once more, I huddled up in a rain coat, hauling rainwater away from the house we could never make a home, flooded internally by the uncertainty of my own identity and future.

9

Ghost

"Are you sure you don't mean dysmorphia?"

"Yes. I'm sure," I asserted. "This is not body dysmorphia. This is gender dysphoria."

The psychiatrist looked at me quite perplexed. I was only seeing him because he was the person I could get in to see the fastest and the Lamictal was running low. Though it's typically indicated for epilepsy, it's also prescribed for bipolar. And more and more that seemed to be the diagnosis the doctors were leaning towards.

This psychiatrist, a stuffy suit with thinning hair, was no exception. He felt a bipolar diagnosis was more accurate than the major depression diagnosis I'd lived with for twenty years. But he wasn't quite as hip to the terms surrounding gender identity.

"I do not have body dysmorphic disorder," I continued. "I know what that is. I don't think my nose is bigger than it is or that my ears are too large. I want to become a man."

"Yes, yes, I understand that. But I believe there's a term for that . . . for the body dysmorphia. That disconnect between your body's actual physical features and what your brain sees."

"It's gender dysphoria! My brain sees a female body because that's what I have, but I loathe it. This is far different than fixating on having a Streisand nose." I was getting livid. But evidently the intensity of my mood was to be expected, given my lovely new solidified bipolar diagnosis. I was hoping maybe the hospital doc had gotten that wrong and my neurologist just went along with it. But this confirmed it. My mom always said if one person tells you that you have a tail, you can probably ignore it. But if five people tell you that you have a tail? You might want to turn around and look.

Everyone was starting to tell me I had a tail, and its name was Bipolar Disorder. It was time for me to turn around and look. I did. I saw it. It was there. But what nobody but me seemed to see was the impact my gender identity was having on that disorder.

This guy wasn't even at the museum, let alone seeing the picture.

"In any case, regarding medication, some people don't always need to be on medication for bipolar. You've had some bad experiences with meds. I wouldn't want to repeat that. We could keep you on a small dose and see how you do, though."

I'd explained that since being on the medication, I'd felt my creativity had dulled, and I was wandering aimlessly through a mental fog. It also felt as if I had cement shoes on while running. I didn't mention the heart skipping, thinking that was an unrelated matter and one I was not yet ready to follow up on.

I was in a weird limbo situation with health care anyway. Since I was not the subscriber on Krissy's policy, I could not get information about people on the plan from the insurance company itself. Krissy was no longer responding to my questions about it.

Her deadline for the house had come and gone. She kept her word and contributed not a penny more. After several calls I finally learned she had dropped me from her insurance coverage as well. I called the state to find out if I could use coverage with them, since Krissy had dropped me. I could.

But my psychologist didn't accept state health care, so I lost a crucial part of my support team for my transition. I searched for a new one as well as a psychiatrist. It turned out I could get in to see Dr. Mercedes— who worked in the same building as I did—more quickly than any other psychiatrist I could find.

And I couldn't find many. Unfortunately, most psychiatrists in private practice don't accept state health care. It's a sad truth about being on welfare. Most doctors don't want to deal with you because they don't get paid as much as they do by private insurance.

My nonprofit employer led me to Dr. Mercedes, who thought he was an expert on all things transgender. I couldn't help but laugh to myself as he tried to explain that I had body dysmorphia but yet reassure me that he truly did understand my condition and had experience treating transgender individuals.

I looked down at the floor and shook my head. "I'd just like the prescription so I can go," I finally said. "How do I taper off this stuff?"

He explained the taper process to discontinue the med and then wished me luck.

I'd be needing it.

THE DULLING OF my creativity coupled with the cinder-block feeling in my shoes was making running an exceptionally difficult activity. After a third fall at full speed and a nice case of road rash, I knew something needed to change. There were too many variables at play, and Lamictal seemed to be at the heart of it. But first I took pictures of my injuries in case I needed to bring up the falling business to my doctors.

I began researching Lamictal and learned that it could cause my foggy brain and lactic-acid-type lethargy. Perhaps that's why I was falling. I was too lethargic and thus catching my toe. The drug needed to go. If I couldn't think during work or couldn't run due to what felt like an impending disruption to my electrolytes (a response I'd had to previous anti-epileptics), then what was the benefit of staying on the medication? It was stealing what little I had left to enjoy in life, not to mention challenging my ability to function cognitively at work.

So with the psychiatrist's blessing, I tapered off. Soon the fog began filtering out of my brain, and the lethargy lessened. To my surprise, the weird skipping in my heartbeat also ceased. Nothing felt amiss. But it didn't change my gait.

"Are you limping?" "Did you injure yourself?" "What did you do to your leg?" The questions seemed to come at me daily. I didn't want to talk about it. I had too much on my plate to consider the reasoning behind my falls.

I was driven by tunnel vision.

Nothing—not even the possibility of the active progression of my neurological disorder—was going to stop me from moving forward with my goal to become a man. But the disconnect between my legal name and how I presented myself was starting to create problems in the workplace. It was already a struggle to work with my employer on disability accommodations.

"I have a special chair," I'd told them during my hiring process. "It's a Herman Miller Aeron chair. I've seen a few around the building here. I can bring mine in, but if you can provide one, that would be ideal."

"Don't bring your chair in," they said. "We'll get you one."

Weeks later, there was still no word on a chair, so I brought mine in and busted out the masking tape to label it with my name. But what would I label it? Outside of work, I was going by Nate again. But employment is often the final frontier for someone who is trans. As of this writing, it's still perfectly legal in many states to fire someone from their job simply because they are transgender. Thankfully, I knew Minnesota had laws that specifically prohibited discrimination based on gender identity.

The law was on my side. Supposedly.

"I'm just afraid this is gonna make it harder than it already is in the workplace," my mom repeated. At some point I flat out told her I needed to take the risk. That it was too painful to continue to pretend to be Jen.

She was nothing more than a ghost.

Each day it became more difficult to hide my identity. I was starting to slip up and call myself Nate. More and more I felt I was living a lie again, a clichéd "double life." But that's precisely what it was.

During the day I passed as an androgynous female, thanks more to my feminine jaw line than any specific accoutrement. I didn't wear makeup or feminine clothes. But the name, pronouns, salutations. I couldn't stand them. I didn't feel like Jennifer, a "she," or a Ms. I didn't identify with who that person even was anymore. As far as I was concerned, Krissy had been right: Jennifer died during the suicide attempt. Nate was born. But he was having a difficult birth. To integrate my identity, I had to take the leap and come out at work. I had to let go of my ghost.

I stared down at my special office chair, contemplating what name to write on the masking tape. Before writing anything, I emailed my boss and IT to formally request my name badge, email, and name plate be changed to reflect my preferred name. I qualified the request, noting that I understood I could not yet change any legal documents in HR or anywhere else. Eventually, I told them, I would change my name legally.

I got no reply.

During that same time, I became eligible for my employer's health care coverage. Though the premiums were manageable, the out-of-pocket max was high. Without enough money, I wouldn't be able to afford to get out of the house if it sold. It was still in show condition as I fought frantically against my wallet and the clock to present the house—and my body, my own home—as being on stable ground.

I RETURNED TO my full-time job on a Monday after working the weekend at Gables, where I'd been moved into a role doing life enrichment with residents with dementia. I came out there as Nate, too, but was met with a much different message.

Gretchen, who had seen my potential and trained me into my role, was the first colleague I talked to about my—until then—shameful little secret. We'd connected in a way I hadn't connected with other coworkers. There was a trust, a camaraderie formed through our mutual passion for seeing the ability in disability, honoring the elderly, and even shared musical interests. At some point, I mentioned my book, which, since I was still playing the role of Jen, was easier to discuss. With that, I disclosed my suicide. The fact that Krissy left. My history of chemical dependency and brain injury. But it was my gender that was the toughest secret to reveal to my new colleague.

It was going to happen whether she approved or not. Why not risk it? I had to start somewhere. To my surprise, she didn't respond with disgust or shock. Her wide eyes narrowed slightly as she began to nod, impressing upon me a look of acceptance and tolerance that seemed authentic, genuine. It also empowered me to go forth to the administration.

I deleted my fears and finally pressed send on an email, fully anticipating pushback from higher ups. Instead, they were happy to change my email and my name badge for me. Happy to provide support. The first time my supervisor saw me in person after receiving my coming out email, she pulled me into a room to talk. "I just want you to know—I think what you're doing is just, it's just awesome. So you," she twirled her hands more than usual to emphasize importance, "you just go, go be you . . . but if anyone gives you a hard time? You just come see me." She pointed her index finger back at herself. The words stuck. The action stuck. She meant it. She'd stand up for me. And that meant the world to me. But I couldn't keep myself closeted at my full-time job any longer. I was dying inside. My boss had tossed a curled piece of label-maker paper in my direction and told me to affix it to the back of the chair. "PROPERTY OF JENNIFER CANNON." I couldn't stand seeing it there.

I pulled the sticker from the chair, leaving behind a sticky residue. I went into my email settings and changed my name in my profile. I grabbed that good ol' masking tape and wrote "NATE" on a piece, shredding it away from the roll as if reclaiming the identity I'd lost as a youth. I taped one piece over my first name on my name badge and another over my first name on my name plate, then affixed a new label to the chair.

The ugly faded beige masking tape stuck out like a sore thumb. Eyes like slits panned from the tape to me and back again to the tape. There went an eye roll. A disgusted shake of the head. A disgruntled sigh.

I wondered why they weren't being written up for that. After all, I'd just been written up for sighing. Yes, sighing.

Six weeks into my employment I was told I could "go a long way" in the organization. But then I disclosed a disability and came out as Nate. I could feel the evil stares shoot out like laser beams from below the furrowed eyebrows of management as they walked by. I was pissing them off, and I knew it. I didn't care. This was my life, and these were my rights. And I was done getting stepped on and dead-set on becoming the strongest me I could become.

I KNUCKLED DOWN in pursuit of chest surgery and testosterone therapy. I'd been given a letter of support for chest surgery from the hotshot gender psychologist I'd seen in 2011, but he still—despite my suicide attempt and ongoing struggles with my gender—would not approve me for testosterone. My psychologist, Mindy, whom I still couldn't see because she didn't take the very unique plan my employer subscribed to, was willing to write me a letter in support of both.

But to get approval for surgery, I'd need letters from two doctors. The time had come to finally call for an appointment with a doctor I'd heard through my internet travels was supportive of transition and not a gatekeeper: an ob-gyn who worked with transgender patients. Still wrestling with some aspects of internal shame regarding my condition, I picked up the phone to request an appointment with Dr. Thorp.

"She has a very lengthy wait list," the woman on the phone said, "but leaves appointment slots open for new patients. Can you come in next week?"

"Yes!" I didn't even need to know the day or time available. I didn't care. Whatever time it was, I was going to make it. And I did. I landed in her office and brought in a stack of medical records regarding my dystonia, mental health, suicide attempt, and gender. She listened with open ears and an open mind. All the while, as I explained my situation and my hopes to start testosterone, I wrestled a subtle shakiness inside. What if she, too, was unwilling to support me on this because of the complexities of my case? She was my final hope. But what doctor would risk putting their patient on a hormone that could potentially magnify brain dysfunction?

I prepared myself for rejection, expecting her to say no, to tell me this would never be an appropriate treatment given my other health issues.

She sat silently, saying very few words as I explained my history, looking over the wire rim of her glasses with a warm smile framing her face. I wound down from my race-car-paced speech and took a deep breath before connecting with her eye to eye.

"So here I am. After all that. It's been a long road, and I've run into nothing but roadblocks. I know what I want. I know who I am. But I need your help to get there."

Her smile widened as she sat up straight and kicked one leg over the over, tucking her blond hair behind her ear. "You've been through enough," she said. "Too much. If you're ready to get started on testosterone, then let's get you started."

An unexpected smile exploded across my face. "Thank you. Thank you so, so much. And the surgery? Would you be willing to write a letter of support? I've got the one from my psychologist, but I'd rather not have the second be from that gender psychologist."

She smiled again, as if she knew a secret. Perhaps the gender psychologist's reputation preceded him. "I'd be happy to write you one," she said. "I'll get that done yet this week, and we'll put it in the mail so you can start moving forward. In the meantime, let's discuss testosterone: what it will do *to* you and what it will do *for* you."

I nodded. Words came out of Dr. Thorp's mouth, but very few stuck. " . . . may experience weight gain . . . keep working out . . . raises your risk of blood clots . . . will elevate cholesterol . . . hairline may recede . . . need to take calcium . . . bones become weaker." She spewed forth the long list of risks and side effects as I paid little attention, too occupied by the film reel of happy images akin to those in a drug commercial floating through my head. She then explained what I could expect in terms of changes.

My period would stop, my voice would drop, and my shoulders would broaden while my hips would narrow. I'd grow more body hair and facial hair. The tissue that comprises the clitoris would grow into what would look like a small penis. My jaw would widen, and an Adam's apple would form.

"We'll need to monitor your levels closely, especially given your history of brain injury and anger. What you're basically going to be doing is going through menopause at the same time as adolescent male puberty."

That sounded like an awful combination, but I didn't care. The costs and risks associated with gender transition would be high, but not transitioning had—and still could—cost me my life.

I'D DONE MY research. I knew which chest surgeons took insurance and which didn't. With my letters of support in hand, I also knew my first call had to be to my insurance company, to find out if surgery would be covered in the first place.

At that time, state health care in Minnesota would not have paid for my gender reassignment. Private insurance was a better bet but still hit or miss. With all the pieces in place, I called Blue Cross Blue Shield while on lunch break and began speaking to a representative.

"What can we do for you, Ms. Cannon?"

I chuckled. Gender was everywhere.

"Can you tell me if gender reassignment services are covered or if they are a policy exclusion?"

The directness of the question crippled her response. "Uhh, oh. Well. I . . . let me look into that for you." A series of questions beginning with "Do you" or "Are you" followed. I had two letters; I had been through therapy; I was out as a man; I was approved to start hormones. What else could they want?

After minutes that dragged on for hours, the woman returned to the line with her nasally twang. She seemed to have an answer.

"It appears that, yes, those services would be covered under the plan," she said.

I shook a fist triumphantly. I wasn't out of the woods yet, though. The insurance company might cover the services, but the employer didn't necessarily have to agree to that. Many employers list gender reassignment services as exclusions to the plan they sponsor for their employees. I had to check, to be sure.

"Okay, so this is covered under the plan I'm subscribed to, correct?"

"Yes."

"Does the employer list any policy exclusions to the plan? If so, are gender reassignment services listed as one of those exclusions?"

The woman again seemed to stammer for a reply. She clarified her understanding of my question before putting me on a Kenny G break. Time ticked faster. My thirty-minute lunch break was nearly up, but I needed this answer. I'd waited years for this moment.

I got out of my car and started back towards the building to clock back in. Perhaps I'd have to call back for my answer. I reached out an arm to the entrance door when the music on the other end of the line stopped.

"Are you still there?"

"Yes, yes I am," I darted a few steps out from under an awning and back out into open sky in search of a slightly better phone signal.

"I am afraid that, yes, gender reassignment surgery is listed as an employer-based policy exclusion. The services would therefore not be covered."

10

Plunge

I was done playing around.

If insurance (correction: my own employer) wouldn't cover it, then I'd just have to take out a loan. Of course, the idea of taking out a $10,000 loan to cover a double mastectomy and chest reconstruction didn't seem all that wise, but it was a sound decision given my situation. I didn't have the money I would need to move when the house sold. That, too, would have to go on a credit card. A loan would have a much better interest rate.

I'd done my research on loans and on the process of gender transition. It's complicated. It involves medical issues with very specific and limiting legal elements. It draws in psychology due to the ridiculous fact that it remains a diagnosable mental illness. It's not easy to navigate any sort of path through the maze that is transition, but I plotted my course. As the rains settled down in June, the flooding in the basement stopped. The house began to show more frequently, and I settled into a groove, forging my path to becoming a man.

FIRST I CALLED the University of Minnesota, where I've been a patient for my neurological disorder since 2009 and had a quote for chest surgery from 2011. Once more, I found myself in my car during a lunch break at work, making health care–related calls. I dialed the number and spoke with the same secretary I'd spoken with the year before. Surely the cost had gone up since then.

She finished up telling me about the fee breakdown.

"So all together, her fee would be $8,000."

Her wording was a red flag. The university has affiliations with a hospital system. It's complicated and beyond the scope of my knowledge how these entities are intertwined. All I know is that as a patient, it often creates two bills. I had to know if my interpretation of her statement was correct.

"So hang on here. The $8,000 would be the doctor and university costs only?"

"Correct. The quoted figure is for the doctor's time and surgical fee."

I got it. That meant the time in the hospital, going under anesthesia, and everything else the hospital would be doing were not accounted for.

The call confirmed it: the doctor at the U was not the right surgeon for me. Years later I'd learn that other trans guys were being charged up to $35,000 for the same surgeon's procedure due to hospital fees.

I CARRIED ON with my jobs, kept the house up for show, and spent much of what little free time I had working on my transition efforts.

I'd heard great things about a guy named Garramone down near Fort Lauderdale. Krissy and I had even gone so far as to ask about basic pricing back in 2011, after learning insurance wouldn't cover it. I also found a retreat for trans guys who go to Florida specifically to get their chest surgery done by this man, who is unquestionably one of the best surgeons in the field. The more I learned, the more I realized the only way I was going to be able to get surgery done was if I stayed at that retreat.

I was single now and had very few friends. And even less family support. I certainly didn't have anyone willing to travel with me.

Double mastectomy and chest reconstruction is not a terribly serious surgery, but it is pretty major in terms of limitations imposed on your daily life. You certainly can't drive home, even though it can be done at same-day surgery facilities. And you can't lift your arms above shoulder level or lift any weight over five pounds for several weeks postsurgery. For that reason, this private-pay surgeon in Florida would only accept patients if they had a safe way to drive away from the facility and be cared for in the days that followed. The retreat offered just that option.

When I broke down the numbers, the entire cost for the surgery, including all surgical and hospital fees, airfare, plus staying a week at a retreat in a mansion, was still less expensive than the $8,000 fee quoted by the university hospital. Not only would staying in Minnesota to have it done at the university possibly result in a bill far greater than quoted due to unknown hospital fees, but it could also mean that a resident might end up being the one to take a scalpel to my chest.

Though it's not a cosmetic procedure, I've never planned on having this surgery done more than once. It's sort of a one-and-done deal. You might be able to redo implants, but you can't undo a mastectomy. I wanted to get this right the first time and make my chest look as much like a man's as possible.

Garramone's website spelled it all out and told me what I'd need to have in place in order to get the process started. I had the letters. I had the money from the loan. I'd found a place to stay. All I needed to do was book a date.

On a springlike sunny Monday in early summer, I took a brief break from my station to step outside. I couldn't wait until lunch. I'd made my decision Saturday and was becoming preoccupied to the point of distraction. With Garramone's office number added to my contacts, I pulled my cell from my pocket and made the call I'd been waiting to make for two years.

Finally, I could schedule surgery.

All I had to lose was nearly everything, including my own life, to get there.

A PERKY WOMAN with a rising vocal inflection answered. I smiled. Her enthusiasm seemed either more genuine than the secretary at the university or perhaps more superficially sellable. Either way, she seemed to be in the right role.

"Hi, um," I'd thought so hard about what to say that all the words were erased from my mental whiteboard as soon as she said the words "Garramone's office." I couldn't believe I was actually calling. A flash of hesitation and shame hit me. As the kids would say, shit just got real.

"I'm, well, I'm transgender, and I want—I need—to start scheduling for chest reconstruction."

"Oh, absolutely! Thank you for calling. I'd be happy to help you get started." Warm and friendly, completely judgment free, the woman took relevant details from me. I was able to provide her with everything she needed in order to get the process moving along.

"Alright, so the next step is that we need you to email us pictures of your bare chest, from the front and both sides." She added a few more specifics about how to hold my arms in the photos. I wasn't so much worried about the arms as the mode of communication.

"Email you pictures of my chest? Wow. That feels risky or risqué or something." I half chuckled out of unease. She didn't.

She explained that the email was only accessed by Dr. Garramone and would only be used for the purpose of evaluating appropriate surgical technique. It was enough explanation for me. Besides, I realized, who cared if people saw my tits now? I was getting rid of the things anyway.

I agreed to send the pictures, which were more difficult to take by myself than I had imagined. I finally settled on the delay timer on the camera Krissy's mom had bought us but that Krissy had left behind. With it, I snapped the requested images and emailed them off to the doctor.

A few days later, he replied and requested we speak by phone to discuss how he'd like to proceed. We arranged the day and time, which couldn't come soon enough. During my now familiar lunch-break phone call, he asked questions about my neurological condition, orthopedic issues, and addiction history. He factored that in as he talked swiftly and seamlessly about the procedure and recovery. His words seemed to flow from the phone directly to my memory.

"I'll have my assistant call you to schedule the procedure," he said. "We may have to be a little more cautious with you, given your condition and your history, but I think you'll be pleased with the results." His tone and obvious intelligence made him easy to trust. So, too, did his reputation.

I LET MY mom know that I'd gotten the surgery scheduling process rolling. She was worried about me, trying to manage everything on my own, working as much as I was. She was also struggling with the idea that changing my gender meant she was losing her daughter forever.

As was the case for most of my friends and family, my decision was, by this point, harder on others than it was on me. She also had serious concerns about my pursuing surgery from a doctor who doesn't take insurance.

Though my mom and I were never *not* on speaking terms, we had only been speaking superficially. She was concerned about my mental health but wasn't ready to process my gender transition. She still thought it wasn't time yet. It would never be the right time, though. She'd always find a reason to say it should wait.

Ever since I can remember, we'd had a deep connection through conversation. Suddenly it felt as if I couldn't talk to my mom, who had seen me through so much. Still, she did want to know when I got the surgery scheduled. Dr. Garramone had said he was scheduling out to October. It was only late June. Disappointing as that was, I was still eagerly awaiting the call from his secretary to get a firm date and time. I was moving forward. I wanted to share that excitement with my mom.

We spoke in the evening, and I told her the news. At first she questioned me. "Are you sure you know who you're dealing with? I mean, what if this is just some back-alley quack with a butcher knife?"

I laughed. "Mom, I wouldn't do that. I want to get good results. This guy seriously has a rep for being the best in the biz. He's a very good surgeon, and this surgery is all he does."

After I offered to send along links to his website and reviews from previous patients, she was unable to fight me on that point any longer. She had no choice but to accept it. She tried. Her words were supportive. But her tone was stern, resembling how she talked to me when I was an untrustworthy crack addict making very poor life decisions. The only difference now: she wasn't angry with me. She was sad.

We said our good-byes and hung up. As I sat on the front porch of my own home, the unmistakable sounds of summer echoed in the distance as the sun began to set. The stress of my life collided with the serenity of the nature surrounding me. There were no roaring jetliners. Just occasional chirps from birds. The silence and sudden internal solitude swallowed me in vertigo fashion. I snapped back from my momentary daze and lit up a menthol.

I'd been smoke-free for over three years when I finally accepted a cigarette from my burglar boyfriend. After inquiring what brand I used to smoke, he went out and bought that brand. At the time, I was feeling vulnerable. One drag led to the next. One smoke to the next. And then I was back smoking daily. Three a day to be exact. One in the morning. One on the way home from work. One at night.

I snuffed out the butt in a small hole on the second step of the front stoop. It was precisely the circumference of a cigarette. Before I quit in 2008, I jokingly referred to it as the "butt hole" or "ash hole," depending on my mood. It got black from snuffing butts out in it, and neither rain nor snow could wipe it clean. After three years of not smoking, it was returning to the color of the pavement again. I twisted the filter and smooshed it into the concrete as memories tumbled through my mind.

How did I end up on these steps, alone in my home, staring at a "For Sale" sign on my lawn, snuffing out a cigarette butt?

How many times did Krissy and I walk up and down these steps? How often did our friends Molly and Maureen come through that front door? None of them would walk those steps ever again. Not with me sitting on them.

BETWEEN THE MUTUAL friends I'd shared with Krissy, my gender being in flux, and the fact my book was out in the world with my female name on it, I couldn't figure out how to present myself. I couldn't continue to pretend to be Jennifer on the internet when everyone who knew me knew what struggles I was having. Nor could I see my coming out online as being a smooth process. Would people in the dystonia community still see me as an inspiration if they found me out? Would people in the mental health or recovery communities still accept me?

For all the fear of rejection, just as I had before my suicide attempt, it was becoming clear that I needed to come out on social media and be honest about my life changes. With the self-perceived pressure mounting, I decided to do it via a video posted to my Facebook fan page. I'd wrestled with having two personal accounts on that site for some time, unsure whether to keep "Jennifer" around and all her memories and mutual friends. I'd also set up a new account as Nate when I was still with Krissy and was friends with a handful of people there.

It created dilemmas about how to proceed, too. Many of those people who "liked" my author page were also my "friend" on my personal account. They would know via the video I was no longer Jennifer Cannon, yet still be friends with me as Jennifer Cannon. How was I supposed to reconcile that without coming out on my personal page, too?

It would turn out to be a difficult lesson to realize that the complex layers of my identity—particularly my gender and my physical and mental health—would change everything about my peer support system and interpersonal relationships.

Soon after I came out online, Molly backed away from me. We'd been friends for almost fifteen years, and for ten years she and her partner and Krissy and I were best of friends. When I was hospitalized, she emailed me. I had access to my email and limited other sites while in the psych ward. In that email she called me the most amazing person she'd ever met. She'd been a great friend, but she'd also struggled to understand my mental health challenges. I was the first person she came out to as a lesbian when we were in college. She was not one of the first people I came out to when I came out as transgender.

But she knew. Far earlier than I realized.

We'd had our ups and downs, but things seemed to be in a good place. I emailed a few times in the early months after the attempt. She and Maureen invited me over on one occasion. It was awkward for me. I suppose it was equally as awkward for them.

I was lacing up my shoes on my way to leave as they waited by their front door to say good-bye. It felt different to be at their house without Krissy. A heavy silence soaked the air. I felt the need to fill it. "Who knows, maybe the next time you see me I'll have a beard!" I joked.

"I don't think it's gonna happen that fast," Maureen said. I took her words to mean they'd see me again sometime soon (though realistically it takes a trans man about two years to be able to grow a beard, and it may never grow in fully). I thought it certainly wouldn't be two years until we saw each other again. It didn't even occur to me that night that we might never see each other again at all.

Over the months I emailed Molly sporadically. I was used to her delayed responses, but finally she only replied back with one thing: a quote from the Dr. Seuss book *Oh, the Places You'll Go!* I didn't interpret it at first to be anything other than encouraging. Indeed, I had brains in my head and shoes on my feet and I was setting on a journey to repair my own self, to make myself complete. I'd loved that book since my brother John gave it to me as a high school graduation gift soon after my first suicide attempt at seventeen.

I replied and thanked her. But as months passed without any further communication, I began to see that her email was a farewell message. She was wishing me well on my journey but excusing herself from my life.

Just as Krissy had.

I decided to keep only my Nate account on Facebook. Molly and I were friends there and still no communication. At some point, I stopped trying.

Sadly, Molly and Maureen were not the only lesbian friends I'd lose. Slowly, over time, I'd see each of my lesbian friends drift out of my life. My ties to and support from the LGBTQ community were suddenly from the B, T, and Q. The L and the G seemed to be less willing to accept me. I'm not alone in this experience. People in the trans community will often comment that the T gets forgotten: by society at large, by those who are cisgender (meaning they feel their gender matches the anatomy they were born with), and by those who see themselves as gay or lesbian.

Times are changing. Transgender rights are at the heart of a very strong social movement now. I hope it will lead to more acceptance of the trans community within the larger queer community, as well as society in general.

But it's a challenge to figure out how to proceed when you feel you're losing everything just in your efforts to be who you really are. It's hard to be rejected, alienated, abandoned, forgotten. In the days after sharing the coming out video on my Jennifer page, I was unfriended by dozens of people. I switched to my Nate account permanently and hand-picked those friends who came along with me. I was starting to accept myself. If someone else couldn't accept me, they were no longer worth my time.

THE CALL FROM Garramone's office finally came. I got a date. Not with a girl. A date with a knife.

"The first available surgery slot we have is October 4," the perky secretary noted.

I was elated. The waiting hadn't pushed my surgery back any further. I simply couldn't do that date, though. I was starting training for the Twin Cities Marathon, which was taking place just three days later. I'd already contacted the organization that puts on the marathon and asked if I could switch my registration from the name Jennifer and female gender to Nate and male gender. To my surprise, the organizers were happy to accommodate the request. I didn't think they'd be receptive, given that if there was a medical emergency, they'd need to be able to identify me. If I was registered under a name that was not yet my legal name, I could see that being a problem. They, however, saw it as no issue and quickly changed my registration.

It would be my first marathon since Krissy left, and so the first when she would not be on the course. But it would also be the first marathon I'd be running as a male, without a stupid *F* on my race bib, announcing to the world my ascribed gender. So with work, house, and all, I set my sights on finishing a race I never imagined I'd be able to conquer without Krissy's assistance, while working more than full-time, and as a man. Those facts alone inspired me to get up each morning and train.

As hard as it was to pass on the first available surgery slot, I had to schedule the procedure for after the race.

"I'd love to take the first available, but I just can't do the fourth. What do you have the following week?"

"Let's see here . . . he's going to be on vacation." My stomach sank like an anchor. I couldn't handle any more delays. "But we do have October 11 open." Thank God.

I wrote the date out on my notepad in numeric form: 10/11/12.
"I'll take it."

It was set. A date. A time. A place. A surgeon. The finances. The
logistics. Settled. All I had to do was wait. Quite often, in the coming months, I'd find myself mentally commiserating with Tom Petty
about how difficult that can be. As I waited, change began to permeate
through every facet of my life.

ALTHOUGH MY INSURANCE would cover testosterone itself, it would not
cover the needles or syringes. I was astounded when the pharmacy told
me it would cost close to $50 for a ten-week vial. Insurance also refused
to cover the testosterone if my diagnosis was coded under any sort of
transgender service code. Instead, my doctor had to list my diagnosis
as "hypogonadism," a diagnosis still used today to ensure coverage. Regardless of diagnosis, though, the insurance would not cover the supplies to inject the hormone. Because, after all, who needs clean needles?
Thankfully the Transgender Health Coalition's Shot Clinic offered free
supplies to guys like me.

Even so, I was scared to start the hormone. Though I'd had my
prescription in my wallet for a week, I'd come down with a chest cold
and was waiting for that to pass before forever altering the hormonal
makeup of my body.

Once the cough dissipated and the sniffles dried up, I was ready to
take the plunge. I stopped in at the clinic on a Friday after work. Beyond offering supplies, the clinic volunteer staff could help you learn
how to inject the hormone properly. Or if you were not comfortable
sticking yourself with needles, they'd do it for you.

The clinic was tucked quietly in the back area of a coffee shop in
South Minneapolis, a neighborhood I used to associate only with cocaine. Now needles were carrying a whole different meaning to me. I
went in and met a woman named Brandi, a red-headed volunteer RN
who was excited to learn it was my first time at the clinic. We talked a
bit about the cold I was getting over. She thought it was safe to proceed.

I didn't know what to expect with respect to the injection procedure.
What I discovered is that much like with addiction, it's a ritualistic

process. There's a barrel (or syringe) to which a larger needle is attached. That needle plunges into the vial to draw the serum. When the correct level is drawn, the needle is removed from the barrel and replaced by a smaller needle.

There are six sites trans men generally rotate their shots between: the upper arms, the thighs, and the buttocks.

"Over time these shots can create scar tissue," Brandi noted. "So it's important to rotate these sites every week." Her compassion and empathy seemed genuine. I disclosed information about my neurological disorder, addiction history, and bad right shoulder.

"Would it be safe to inject in my right arm, given my shoulder issues?" Brandi couldn't say for sure—after all, she wasn't a doctor. But she could tell me what she thought. And the more we talked, the more we seemed to think a lot alike. Brandi had been a hockey player, was interested in neurology and orthopedics as a nurse, and had a unique interest in transgender issues. We seemed to instantly become friends. Laughing and chatting, we spent more time in the "shot closet" of the clinic than I'd expected, as she explained to me how to cap a barrel, keep the vial sterile, ensure the needle is properly placed in the muscle, and confirm it's not hitting a vein.

Between what little intravenous administration of cocaine and meth I participated in during the course of my addiction, the countless blood tests for drugs, the IVs, and the twenty or so pokes with Botox I get for my dystonia every ten weeks, I'm hardly squeamish about any sort of needle. But I didn't really want another needle introduced into my life. Since it was inevitable, I needed to make sure I was doing it properly.

Brandi would show me how. She walked me through the process step by step. She got the hormone drawn up into the syringe and removed the cap.

"Alright. Are you ready?" Her excitement was radiant.

"I'm as ready as I've ever been—or will ever be," I said. The flip-flop between fear and enthusiasm for taking this leap was resolving itself. I'd continued to take steps. I'd continued to move along with the process. I went to the clinic on my own time, on my own terms. It was beginning to feel as if I was being guided through transition by powers greater than myself.

Much like with addiction, I paused a moment to contemplate. *How the fuck did I end up here?*

But unlike addiction, my brain pulled me back to reality. *You're here not because you're giving into an addiction. You're here to become who you were meant to be. You're here because you are saving your own life.*

The thoughts spun through my brain. Brandi seemed to be able to see them spin. I stared down at my lap and the stack of medical supplies I was now toting. So much had happened to bring me to this point. And once that needle hit my arm, there was no going back. This was it. This was what I wanted.

Brandi came around to my left side, and I pulled up my sleeve. With a single poke, she jabbed the needle into my deltoid muscle by my shoulder. She pulled the plunger back slightly to ensure there was no blood inside the syringe before pushing forward. The plunger moved slowly due to the viscosity and thickness of the hormone. I held my arm still, watching the process. The clear fluid in the syringe was gone, the plunger at zero.

Brandi pulled the needle from my arm and dropped it in a sharps container. She grabbed a gauze pad and massaged the area, to break up the hormone molecules and prevent them from balling up.

"That's it!" she said. "How do you feel? Like a whole new man?"

I smiled with a smirk and a quiet laugh.

"Yeah," I answered. "I do. I really do."

11

Love and My Rage

The summer nights whirled by in a blur with the house showing daily. I decided to visit Los Angeles in July, to meet a woman I'd been talking with online. It was a desperately needed escape from the house, work, and Minnesota in general. Though it seemed the communities I had previously been involved with no longer wanted much of anything to do with me, some exceptionally accepting people were popping into my life. Brandi was the first. Heather was the next.

She was a single mom in recovery from addiction, and we realized soon after meeting that we made much better friends than partners. I awoke in the hotel the morning after I arrived; Heather and her son, Alex, were still fast asleep in the next bed. Alex, not quite a year old, jostled awake. He gave a wailing cry, foreign to my ears, and I put my index finger to my lips. Heather opened an eye and looked up.

"Sorry," I whispered. "I'll go get some breakfast so you can sleep."

"Wait." She sounded groggy. "Can you take Alex? I rarely get a chance to rest, and he's not gonna go back to sleep now." In fact he was still crying.

"Sure," I said. The words exuded confidence, but inside I was feeling unsure of my fitness for the task.

Once dressed and ready, Alex was cool and calm as I carried him to the elevator, and then from the elevator to the breakfast room. By the time I got there, my dystonia was rebelling, causing my muscles to quiver in tremor-like fashion, tugging at the fibers and pulling me to adopt a posture not conducive to holding a child. I fought against it but was losing my grip.

"How does your mommy do this, Alex? My gosh." I scurried towards a table and transferred him to a proper seat.

"Whew," I said, pulling a sippy cup from the small bag Heather had also sent with me. "That's a workout!" I've never had any intention of being a parent, but I realized then that even simple tasks most parents do could be very difficult with my condition. I felt confident in the forward movement of my gender transition; it was not my gender that was impairing my life. It was right back to the limitations posed by my disability.

Just as it had been years ago.

COFFEE BROUGHT ME to attention as I turned my thoughts to breakfast. The spread was unremarkable, but there's something about Belgian waffle makers. They become irresistible when placed in hotels. With Alex settled in with a bowl of Cheerios, I watched my waffle timer, drifting off in thought about the life I was trying to build for myself. My efforts to feel at home.

I'd never been to California before, but as soon as I arrived, I felt at home. I didn't feel gawked at or talked about by passersby. I didn't have flashback memories of my suicide attempt every time an HCMC ambulance rolled by because there were no HCMC ambulances. In fact, there were no physical markers of my past. No downtown skyline that now only reminded me of the paralegal career I had and lost. No lakes or trails that looked more like a memory book of time spent with Krissy than geographical features.

There were no memories in LA. There was only what millions of others have seen in California: hope for a new life—a life with sunshine, opportunity, and accepting communities. At the time, Minnesota was trying to ban same-sex marriage via the state constitution while California was trying to legalize it.

A tinny ding reminded me my waffle was done. I flipped it over, flopped it to the plate, and thought about what I'd brought with me to California: running clothes, casual clothes, beach clothes, and my body. My still female body—disguised by my male appearance and expressions.

You can't get on a plane or rent a car without legal identification. Just after I arrived at LAX, a woman at the rental car counter took my ID. I headed to the bathroom after finishing with her and panicked, realizing she could probably still see me and probably knew I was still technically a woman. The restrooms marked a fork in the road: the men's room and the women's room. I started to the women's room out of panic when the janitor hollered at me.

"Hey," he said. I spun around. "That's the women's room, man." He cocked his head quizzically, splashing his mop back in his bucket.

"Ha! Yeah. Silly me." The capillaries on my smooth facial skin widened, letting the red seep in above my still narrow, feminine jawline.

He'd read me as a male. I was thrilled, especially since just minutes earlier the shuttle driver had read me as female. The woman at the counter seemed unsure, so just went by what was on my ID. But thanks to the janitor, I knew which direction to go. I had headed west, and out there I felt welcome to head right into the men's room.

The waffle was crispy on the edges but tough. I decided to rip it apart with my hands rather than monkey with plastic silverware. Perhaps the testosterone was making me more primitive. It sure was making me hungrier.

I doused the shredded waffle in syrup and sat down at the table with Alex, who was occupied with his sippy cup and a now spilled bowl of Cheerios. He pushed the Os around his tray in between sips. I demolished my waffle. As I savored a bite drenched in syrupy sweetness, my phone rang.

It was the realtor. What an awkward time for a phone call. I answered with a food-muffled hello.

"Jennifer!" he said. The emphatic way he spoke my female name was always so jarring, as if he'd been holding his breath while the phone rang, just waiting to blurt it out enthusiastically as soon as I answered. "I have great news."

"Really?" I was still chewing, moderately frustrated that I had to be Jennifer in dealing with him. Never mind the fact that he seemed to enjoy emphasizing my female name, even though I'd told him I was transitioning and would prefer to be called Nate. I picked up my coffee to hasten the waffle swallow. *I should be paying attention*, I thought. *This is important.*

Indeed.

"I'm sorry, but can you repeat the last thing you just said? I didn't catch that." I hadn't caught much of anything he said.

"I said we got an offer on the house. I think we should take it."

My coffee-logged waffle belly flipped over, as if it, too, had been in the waffle iron. This would turn everything upside down. I was just contemplating all the changes, and now everything else was about to change again.

I didn't know what to say. I asked questions to get more details. He provided them. Alex began to scream.

"I'm sorry," I said. "Just one second." I put the phone down and Alex on the floor, toys in his hands. The reality of where I was sitting settled onto my shoulders as I picked the phone back up. "I want to make this happen," I said. The words came out unexpectedly. "But I'm out of town right now. I won't be back for a few days."

"Well, Jennifer," he said, "I think we gotta jump on this. I mean, this is the opportunity right here. This is your chance to get out of that house and start new. This document requires a signature. We don't want this to slip away."

"Wait a minute. It requires *a* signature? As in, one?"

"Technically, yes, this can be done with one signature. Just as long as you both agree, and we get both signatures in the near future."

"Then can't Krissy sign it? This is the first time I've been out of town since we separated. I want to enjoy this. She's been out of town several times, as I've taken care of 99 percent of the house-selling process. She can do this one."

After much deliberation, he agreed to nudge her to sign. It worked. The house was officially being sold.

AFTER ENJOYING LA, I returned reluctantly to Minneapolis, where life as I knew it seemed to be happening faster than I could keep up.

My friend Brian, who had visited me in the psych ward, had been working for the National Alliance on Mental Illness and told me that they were interviewing for speakers. I was selected, went through training, and started giving presentations around the Twin Cities. It became therapeutic. My book was doing okay. But my full-time job was still draining the life from my soul.

After far too much delay, they finally gave me a mouse, chair, and keyboard tray. It was a step in the right direction. So too was the new name plate and name badge. But something still didn't feel right. I wasn't doing much to help my own cause as my mental health worsened.

It wasn't so much suicidal thoughts anymore, though those are generally ever present and so gauged not by their presence or absence but rather by their magnitude. It was the anger. The anger that felt chemical, raw, physical, primal. It felt unlike any sort of anger I'd ever experienced. In the August heat, I continued training for the marathon, running early in the mornings before work. I was putting in more miles than my plan called for, just to try to sweat the rage out. Sometimes it worked; sometimes it didn't. Usually it was somewhere in the middle. It was a struggle I'd not experienced since getting sober.

Testosterone had started to cause tremendous changes. My period had stopped right away. I was starting to get a rasp in my voice that people usually mistook for a cold. But the physical effects seemed to be fucking with my head. "You're like the Incredible Hulk right now," Brandi told me. "Your hormones are all over the place."

It FELT LIKE it. On a particularly busy day at work, I found myself the lone scheduler in a row of five. The appointments I was scheduling were different from those my peers were doing. I was scheduling sessions for individuals seeking assistive technology, like iPads, to help them speak. It involves legal paperwork as well as the coordination of two very specialized therapists. It was far different—and far more complex—than scheduling a physical therapy appointment for low-back pain.

I stopped my work to look up and see all of my fellow schedulers gone. A woman appeared. I helped her, and she moved along, but the line grew. The man before me had a complaint and some complex scheduling requests from the physical therapist. The heads in line craned to the sides, to look ahead as if in a traffic jam. Only, instead of watching the result of a fender bender, the people in the line were staring at me. Actually, they were *glaring* at me.

I hurried as fast as I could, but the client was struggling with getting his words out coherently. The glares grew more pointed, searing their way into the part of my brain where my anxiety resides. It amplified my inattention. The man talking. The eyes glaring. The clock ticking. Where were my peers?

My irritation grew. My heartbeat quickened. The man kept talking. The eyes kept glaring. The clock kept ticking. People were looking at their watches. They had mobility transportation waiting. I'd make them late if I didn't hurry up. My brain. Off to the races.

Just stay calm. Take a deep breath. I tried thinking my way through it, practicing a little mindfulness. But it didn't work. Somehow I got the man scheduled, yet my rage kept creeping up my neck towards my vocal box, where I was in the process of dropping octaves. I needed to get out of there.

"Excuse me a moment." I smiled at the woman who stepped up to schedule, got up from my chair, and went to the employee bathroom, which was just behind the wall from my desk area.

I closed the heavy door. A loud buzz from the dull fluorescent above the sink was interspersed with the rhythm of my heavy breaths. Beads of sweat began to form on my brow, my back, and my chest. I grabbed my shirt and fanned it against myself as I fought the urge, the pressing, unrelenting urge to completely and utterly freak the fuck out. Scream, yell, thrash, hit things. Lose my shit.

I paced the room, which doubled as a changing room and restroom for patients of the clinics adjacent to physical therapy—the psychiatry and pediatric clinics. The rage, the hate for this horrible job that I was only doing because it was all I could find to keep a roof over my head, hit me.

A deep scream with a range that would have been impossible to attain before starting testosterone bellowed from my soul, roaring as if the man in me had suddenly grown to become a lion. I punched the metal door before settling on pummeling the padded doctor's office bed with both of my fists. With each punch, chunks and splatters of rage left behind an air of palpable intensity.

My energy climaxed, then crashed. I fell to my knees as tears started to mix with sweat.

"What the fuck is *wrong* with me?" I pleaded, putting my palms to my face.

It felt that I stayed there for an eternity, kneeling at the side of the doctor's office bed. But it was probably only a few seconds before I got up to wash my face with cold water and try to rinse the experience away. It wouldn't work. Something told me I probably shouldn't stay in the bathroom much longer.

Upon exit, someone asked me if I was okay. I said I was and returned to my work station and finished out the day.

The next week I got a call from Dr. Thorp's office. Her assistant, Angie, was known to use terms of endearment such as "hon" and "dear" frequently, so it came as no surprise that her voicemail included such words. It was the urgency of her request for me to call that concerned me.

We finally connected. "Dr. Thorp needs to see you right away, dear," she said.

My first question was obvious. "Why?"

"Well, I guess you're just special," she said. "She's even willing to come in at an earlier time to meet with you if work gets in the way."

My first question was obviously much more complicated than I thought. A doctor wouldn't want to urgently see me because I'm "special." All Angie could tell me was that there was a concern Dr. Thorp wanted to talk to me about.

I feared it had something to do with surgery.

My anxiety shivered in the cold room until Dr. Thorp arrived. She thanked me for coming in early and then got right to the point. "So how are ya doin' with the testosterone? Having any trouble with irritability or anger?"

"Why?" Again with my complicated question.

She gave a slight shoulder shrug and slid the question off with a vague response suggesting it was important to know for my dosage.

I, in turn, admitted to nothing of severity. "Maybe a little bit. It feels different, though. It feels chemical."

She nodded as she pulled some papers from her file. "Well, from what I hear, it sounds like it might be giving you more than just *a little* trouble."

"What do you mean?"

"I got a call from a social worker you work with who you've been talking to."

I explained that my colleague was well versed in the complex aspects of state health care. I'd approached her to ask some questions about my situation after she and I began chatting casually. She'd seemed to be worried about me as of late. The stress of the house and my health care costs and working too much when I was going through so much: I guess it was starting to show.

My coworker had heard about the bathroom incident; her office was right down the hall from where my depths-of-hell growl echoed through the walls. She had pulled me in to talk to me a few days later. After telling me how worried she was about me, she started to cry. I can't recall if I cried myself, but I do recall that I was an absolute jerk to her.

I stormed out, angered by what I perceived to be an invasion of my privacy. I'd merely reached out for assistance in finding affordable health care. I never signed up to be therapized by a colleague.

This conversation with Dr. Thorp irritated me. "We talked about health insurance. That's it. I only told her I was undergoing transition so she could understand my situation better."

"She's a mandated reporter. She has to make others aware when she's concerned for someone." Dr. Thorp's words added fuel to my frustration, transforming me into a raging beast. This was not the doctor I could let anger show with, though. I tried to keep it hidden, but it seeped out.

"This really pisses me off," I added.

She knew something was up and, after explaining the legitimacy of my colleague calling out of concern for my well-being, turned her attention back to the papers she pulled from her folder earlier.

"Look right here." She circled a number on the top page and slid it in my direction. I craned my neck, peered down, and saw lab results from a draw I'd had just days before the primal scream episode. On the left was the test name, then a column with my results, followed on the right by the normal range. The number she circled looked to be well within the range of acceptable limits.

"I don't get it. Looks normal to me."

"It's a normal value for women," she said. "But it's way below where we want you to be."

Of course, I was still a woman. Legally anyway. So therefore my labs were normed against values for women. It made sense, but why was this so important?

"Low levels like this can cause all sorts of problems with mood stability and anger," she said.

Pulled from the depths of nowhere, pressure began to stir beneath my eyes. My thoughts, running figure eights as usual, fixated on the fear this would make it impossible for me to continue with hormone therapy. If I couldn't control my anger now, wasn't it only going to get worse as my levels went up? I'd heard all kinds of horror stories about the anger struggles trans men can face because of hormonal imbalance.

"So what does this mean? Are you gonna make me stop taking it?"

Taken aback, she raised her eyebrows in a quick flash. "What makes you think that would happen?"

"Because I have a neurological disorder and psychiatric issues and a history of brain injury and was an addict and have had anger problems and I could go on but—"

She leaned forward with honest eyes. "I'm not gonna make you stop taking it. In fact, this number," she pointed again to the circled digits, "needs to come up. We need to up your dose."

I smiled sheepishly, half embarrassed by my own anxious fears but relieved by my misunderstanding.

"Oh, okay," was all I could mutter.

She went on to explain the dose increase, up to 0.25 milliliter by syringe, once a week. The ritual was becoming routine. Adjusting the dose wouldn't be a problem. In fact, I liked the idea. I wasn't seeing, feeling, or noticing many changes physically yet (apart from the scratchy voice that dropped notes on occasion), but apparently low testosterone was making it difficult for me to manage my emotions. I agreed to the increase.

"You need to be seeing a psychiatrist," she added.

"Meds don't seem to agree with me."

"You still need to be seeing one. I know someone I think you'll really like. She's great; I refer a lot of my patients to her." Dr. Thorp scribbled a few notes then handed me an appointment card. "Her name is Dr. Wiersgalla." It was clear that if I wanted to continue with hormone therapy, I'd need to take care of my mental health.

I left the early morning appointment—set up because I was "special"—feeling special in a way I never imagined. Just to get the doctors' permission to become the person I truly am I had to follow the same orders I'd been given at twelve: see a psychiatrist. I didn't have a choice then. I didn't seem to have a choice now.

It made me want to rebel, to do exactly the opposite of what she told me to do.

"Transsexualism," as it was long referred to in the *Diagnostic and Statistical Manual of Mental Disorders*, is still as of this writing considered to be a mental illness. It was called gender identity disorder for awhile and remains diagnosable under the term gender dysphoria. Nobody I know who is trans uses the word "transsexual" to describe themselves. It's practically a slur. Regardless of what it's called, I don't think it should be considered a mental health diagnosis. I wasn't being sent to a psychiatrist because I was trans, though. I was being sent because I was a trans guy with a history of mental health challenges who was mired in a hormonal, neurological, economical, sociological, psychological, all-out physical battle against a myriad of complex life intersections.

Anyone in my shoes would need a shrink. I didn't want to go. I didn't have time, with all that was going on. Dr. Thorp understood my situation but urged me to consider it before sending me on my way.

I stepped out of the clinic and paused a moment to take in a breath of fresh air. For as apparently serious as my bathroom Hulk roar outburst had been, I was half expecting to finish my appointment by being escorted right into the back of a squad car for a trip to the ward. I most certainly hadn't been expecting to be told to take more T.

12

Closing Time

I considered the offer of psychiatric help but wasn't quite ready to accept it. The hormones were messing with me enough; I couldn't add the weight of some lethargy-laced pill that left me feeling as if I were wearing cement shoes. Thankfully, the hormones started to level off, and so, too, did my emotions.

The summer days blurred by as I spun in the whirlwind. Work, home, health, health insurance, Botox expense, surgery expense, house-related costs, the car, the cat, the second job, the speaking engagements, the book, the business of the book, the bills. Every facet of my life collided together in just a few months.

After much hesitation, I agreed to sign the closing documents on the house. My stipulation was that Krissy had to agree in advance to cover all closing costs. I'd been paying the bills since January, the mortgage since May, plus doing all the prep for showing. She made far more money than I did and could afford to pony up the dough.

She used the fact we were never able to marry so we couldn't legally divorce to her advantage. She was able to take 100 percent of our financial worth, and I had absolutely no legal recourse.

I MERGED ONTO the interstate and was brought to a stop, wedged between an orange construction barrel and another car. With the iconic *Cherry and Spoon* sculpture, which Minneapolis is famous for, just off to my right, my phone rang.

"Jennifer!" The name felt so wrong, so backwards, so abrasive. I didn't correct the realtor anymore. It did no good.

"Hi Lyndon," I said.

He settled into conversation about the closing date. I inched forward in my small black Scion. "This is a delicate sale now, Jennifer. We need to be sure we give the buyers—and Krissy—what they want. Ideally they'd like to take possession mid-September. Krissy wants to go with that."

"Mid-month?" I checked my blind spot. I dislike driving while talking on the phone. Though legal in Minnesota, it shouldn't be.

I explained that mid-month possession would mean I'd have to pay the mortgage, the moving expenses, deposit on a rental, and at least a half month's rent on that rental. That was too much for me to afford.

"If that's the date they're set on and this is, in part, Krissy's wish, then I won't be paying the mortgage or house-related bills for September."

Taken aback once more by my bold stance, Lyndon hesitated, then explained that the sellers usually take care of that. I didn't care. I was on a mission to be more assertive and not be walked on. I certainly wasn't going to be walked on by Krissy. She could pay the mortgage for September rolled into the closing costs. I gave her no choice but to do just that when September rolled around and I didn't pay it.

By that point, I'd had to get it figured out: find a way to get out of the house and settled into a new place to live. Find a way to get my surgery scheduled and done. Find my true self.

With every day creeping closer to my surgery, I was starting to see changes on T. My voice was dropping. My Adam's apple was growing, facial hair starting, and jaw becoming broader, more pronounced. I was feeling refreshed, starting to find myself, and in desperate need of a new environment as I hit the peak of training for my first marathon as a man, with a moving truck and the closing date fast approaching.

My brother John, who, unlike my brother Craig, was still in my life, helped me do some packing. He always had been a model big brother. My situation frustrated him, though. He offered what he could, assisting with the physical aspects of packing up my life and possessions, sorting through Krissy's shit and the like. His wife, Vanessa, helped out as much as she could as well, given she'd just had surgery. My friend Marie also helped, but it was clear she was starting to drift away.

At the end of the day, though, when I put my head down on the same pillow, on the same bed that I shared with Krissy for so many years, I was still alone, mangled by memories.

To STAY STABLE, I focused on my future as Nate. Perhaps that future didn't include many of the people from my past. The present was chaotic enough. During our meeting about the Hulk episode, Dr. Thorp ordered me off work for two days longer than my surgeon's letter stated.

"This won't sit well with them," I told her.

"Well, can you file for short-term disability or FMLA?"

"I haven't been with the company long enough."

"I'm still ordering you off work for an additional two days." She looked me square in the eyes and leaned closer. "They have to listen to that."

"Yeah, but they're gonna find a way to fire me. I know they will." Much the way I would have approached things at age five, I seemed to be having a case of the "yeah-buts."

She assured me we'd cross that bridge if and when we came to it. Unfortunately, we were barreling head on towards that bridge with a brick on the gas pedal. I knew everything in that area of my life was going to crash. I could feel it coming.

I'd felt it before. I was sensing it again. I wanted to get out of my job, but there was no sense in leaving before surgery. I had enough PTO saved up to cover my time off, so I pushed through. I was also pushing through some of the longest runs of the Twin Cities Marathon training season. In fact, my twenty-mile run, what is traditionally referred to as the "long run" that caps off most marathon plans, was set to fall on moving day. I'd booked a truck. I was set to go, ready to move into a one-bedroom apartment just west of the perpetually trendy Uptown area by Lake Calhoun.

I'd take possession, clean it up, and make it feel like home. A few days later a truck would come to the house and transport the remnants of my broken life. The items would emerge from the truck at the destination as symbols of a new beginning. Or at least that's how I imagined it all would go.

Instead, I was living in fear of losing my job before I was even able to prove my ability to live independently. But just to get to moving day I'd have to get through a meeting with HR. I'd emailed the letter from Dr. Thorp to my supervisor, Erin, as well as the director of HR, Katrina. They responded by calling me in.

Vertical windows lined the conference room on the second floor, overlooking the warm-water therapeutic pool. Katrina and Erin stood back, Katrina extending her arm forward to allow me first choice of seat at the long table surrounded by a dozen chairs. I looked out and down at the pool where people, some with conditions far more serious than mine and some not nearly so, exercised for therapy. My disability. My gender. I wouldn't dare do pool therapy at that point in my transition, even though it had been suggested. The things people take for granted.

I walked around to the far side of the table and pulled my stare away from the waters below to take a seat. Erin sat down with her usual straight-backed proper form. Katrina closed the door as if there were a need to whisper and then followed suit. These were women who, in everyday life, I would have absolutely nothing to do with. We had nothing in common.

Yet here on the corporate ladder, they had complete control over my entire financial well-being via my employment status.

The sound of my own anxious breath felt amplified in the silence.

Katrina tucked her hair behind her ear and cleared her throat, by-passing the formalities. "I don't have to approve this request you know."

"Why is that?"

"Because your taking time off for this reason is no different than me taking time off to remodel my house."

I put a hand to the underside of my chin, a sensory trick that helps my dystonia, just to keep my jaw from falling to my lap. "So wait a minute," I said, pausing and leaning back, "are you likening my gender reassignment surgery to a cosmetic improvement to a structure?"

She put her hands to the glossy-topped wooden table, nails clicking upon the impact of each forthcoming syllable. "I . . . don't have to ap-prove . . . this request." Her slow enunciation of the phrases grated my ears as much as the tap of her fake nails.

"This is a medically necessary procedure. This is not cosmetic." Trying desperately to keep a lid on my anger and remain professional, I seemed to be losing a bit of breath. The urgency and desperation trying to pour out of me pressed on my vocal box, my tongue, my mouth. My preoccupation with holding back took me out of the conversation.

"This could put undue burden and undue hardship on the department," I heard. I knew that language—that term—from my time as a paralegal. My legal brain woke up.

"It's for a medically necessary procedure, and my doctor is recommending this additional time due to my neurological condition." I could think of no other defense. Except mentioning my colleagues. "Kim took a week off and then some to go on vacation, and that wasn't questioned. This is for medical reasons."

"I don't want to hear about medical reasons when the fact is that this time off could create undue hardship. I *am* going to approve your request." She got up from her chair, as did Erin, who had been silent through much of the conversation. "But any additional days will be a hardship and can't be guaranteed." They headed to the door as I stood up from my chair.

Katrina turned back around to look at me once more, shaking her blond hair over her shoulder. "You're on thin ice here," she said. "Really thin ice."

My fears were coming true. They were determined to find a way to drive me out.

FOUR A.M. UP on time. Ready to go. I awoke the morning of moving day and headed out for a twenty-mile run. The drag in my right leg was my toes not clearing the ground all the way. When things really went wrong, down I went. The pain for the most part was absent in my lower right leg, but my hip was definitely starting to feel the gnawing effects. In fact, a lot of my bones were crawling with ache.

I pressed on through the miles anyway, energized by the sunrise and mired in that space between disbelief and celebration. My hopes for leaving that house once and for all were finally becoming reality. No more airplane noise. No more old-house problems. No more money pit.

But as my run ended, sentimentality opened up. This would be the last time I'd ever step out the side door of the first home I owned. The last time I'd head out on these streets for a run. Mental photo streams reeled through my mind: from the excitement of the time we first toured the home to the times it brought out the worst in both of us. I was leaving behind a chapter of my life. I just never thought I'd be leaving it in such fashion.

With the final shower, another glimpse of my chest. I didn't even want to look at it. Surgery was just three weeks away. The marathon, work dilemma, surgery, and desperate yearning to make my body match my self. The stress was all too much. I couldn't let myself process my gender anymore. I only knew one thing: in order to rebuild, I first needed to tear down the walls of my life—shower curtain and all. Hook by hook, I unclasped the curtain and liner, still damp from the final drops of water from my last shower in my first house.

The last time. For so many things.

The last time I'd brush my teeth in that sink. Put my contacts in using that mirror. The same sink, same mirror, where memories of my first questioning my 34Bs came to surface after all those years of silence. The same mirror stared back at me the reflection of a person more and more resembling a man—a person I both longed to be but at the same time barely recognized. I entered that home a lesbian in a committed relationship. I was leaving there a single man.

I looked at my reflection one last time before a knock at the door alerted me that my moving help had arrived. Then the truck with the men. So the cat got put in the bathroom. The boxes started moving. Chaos ensued.

Everything had been packed up in boxes for months. Taking up metaphorical space, the boxes seemed to suggest that my life still occupied this larger space called a house. A house that I still technically owned. The boxes were moved, leaving behind empty space. Piece by piece, out the door until every last lamp and every small box were tucked neatly away in a truck and two cars. Ferrick and I took our seats in my coupe. I started it up, trying not to let my emotions do the same, and set off on my way, running in a new direction.

Albeit, a bit slower. Dr. Thorp had increased my testosterone dosage, and I was starting to feel the effects. No more Hulk-like rage episodes. That was a positive. So, too, was the reestablishment of some sense of emotional stability. At the peak of marathon season, though, it was not great timing for the increased dose to add a heavy, weighted lethargy to my stride.

As the weeks diminished to days leading up to the race and the plane ride to Florida thirty-six hours afterward, I settled into my new place. My own place. Working two jobs, seven days a week, to pay my own rent and rebuild my life from square one.

Just me and Ferrick. My little buddy was by my side as I grew into my new identity and cherished my new space, the space I'd looked at when it was vacant and immediately thought, *This is perfect.* Freshened with brand-new beige carpet that thickened the air with glue, a sunken living room led to a screened-in porch, while a large walk-in closet gave way to a spacious bedroom. It had everything I needed. And wanted.

In some ways, it became my bachelor pad. I was in no place for a relationship. I was finding myself, and this was a journey I was intent on taking solo. Only my cat was welcome to sleep in my bed.

As race day crept closer, I picked up my packet with the name Nate Cannon on it. It would be my first marathon as a man. I packed my bags for Florida a few nights before the race, knowing I'd be a bit lethargic afterwards. Not so much from the miles but from sitting at a desk all day the day after the big event.

After 26.2 miles on my feet and some 1,500 miles in the air, I set foot down in Fort Lauderdale. Ready for the pre-op. And ready to go under the knife.

13

Pre-Op

The black town car arrived only after I'd been told to board the wrong van, been driven around a ritzy area of Fort Lauderdale, and then returned to the airport by a supremely angry driver. Evidently, allowing me to board the wrong vehicle was a big no-no. I sat awkwardly on the rear bench-style seat of the shuttle van as the driver cursed himself in Spanish and punched at the steering wheel, screeching recklessly around tight turns crammed with pedestrians. The town car was the right car, sleek and smooth. We left the airport and the angry driver behind.

The next stop was some other guy's drop-off. A hotel, up the interstate a couple dozen miles from Fort Lauderdale. Further on, my destination. A swanky mansion resort in a gated community outside Delray Beach, giant front doors and all. After meeting my hosts, I found my way to my room and then to the pool out back.

The memories tugged at me, but I wanted to stay present. Be in the moment. Enjoy being in Florida. And in a weird way, much like my mom, I needed to mourn. Jennifer would legally still linger but soon cease to exist in physical form. Despite the other changes, from the voice drop to the shoulders broadening, I still had breasts. Without them, I would no longer have that incongruence staring me in the face after every shower. I'd no longer have to hide them. Yes, I'd be given the affidavit stating I was now biologically male, but more importantly for my mental health, I'd finally be free of the flesh that had come to feel so foreign.

The backyard pool made it easy to pass the time. The soft drip of the fountain off the side of the deep end created a soothing background as I skimmed the pages of my mental memory books. Soon the other guests returned. I examined the group and quickly realized I was the only one there without a partner. I'd not yet found anyone I'd connected with romantically and was determined to both embrace and carry out this journey of transition as a single, independent man. In the presence of so many happy couples, surrounded by partners who were supportive of their loved ones' transition, it was hard not to think about Krissy. It had been ten months since the breakup. Is that enough time to recover from the betrayal of a ten-year commitment?

Adding to the bitterness over seeing supportive partners was the fact that I was older than the others. Not only did this mean that many of them still enjoyed partying, but it also meant I was sucked into the negativity cesspool that can be my own mind. *If only I had been able to transition when I was younger,* I thought. Or, *If only I'd been born a generation later.*

The differences between myself and the other retreat goers were far greater than our similarities. We together made a grocery store run and settled in for our pre-op appointments, which for most were scheduled for the following day. I was one of those. But I was scheduled last, late in the afternoon.

There was, conveniently, a mall located across the street from Garramone's office, which was a significant drive from the resort. All those with appointments once again boarded the minivan. Those with afternoon appointments spent the morning at the mall and vice versa. As soon as we arrived, the others broke off into their pairs. I shopped alone, unashamedly, willing to walk into any men's store in the mall and spend a few dollars on new attire.

With my body changing so rapidly, I was fast outgrowing my old clothes. My wardrobe was limited further by the fact that since starting to present as a man, I had fewer clothes to choose from. Yet here I stood, about to become a biological man.

It was about time I had clothes to match.

IT'S HARD TO find clothes that fit me—I'm five foot two, but my torso was lengthening, hips narrowing, angles changing. My body was undergoing incredible changes. My shirts were fitting differently, and I was struggling to wear many of the clothes I could trust for years to fit me. I did, after all, wear a lot of men's clothes before transition. Those were fitting better. But the women's clothes that were passably androgynous were quickly becoming too short in the torso, too narrow in the shoulders, too short in the sleeves. My body was exploding with muscle, hormones raging through both the normal and the dystonic tissue where I'd injected it every seven days religiously for three months. In the end a zip-up sweater and two short-sleeve Ts joined my collection as I celebrated for the first time in my entire life being able to confidently walk into a mall and shop freely in the men's section.

A smile was definitely in order as I strolled in to my afternoon appointment. The small clinic, unremarkable from the outside, shone with glossy black marble floors and counters, postmodernism oozing from every corner of the office. The secretary, a perfectly tan blond woman with teeth whiter than paper, extended an enthused greeting.

"You must be Nate," she said. I nodded. "Great. We'll get you all set up here. But first, some paperwork to sign."

I filed through the stack. I thought I'd given them everything but the keys to my car to get this far, but apparently they still needed more. I complied, sat back down on another round-back chair, and waited. Before I even became uncomfortable, the shiny secretary called me back to an exam room. Words were said, but only my eyes were at attention. Full-length mirrors covered one wall. The black exam chair positioned artfully in the opposite corner complemented the marble counters to the left, where cold, sharp medical instruments lined up methodically like soldiers in a doctor's brigade.

I couldn't help touching the handles of the scalpels. How much power there must be in being able to take such a tool to another living creature's body. It energized me. This man was good with these tools, and he knew what to do. This was costing a pretty penny, but as I caught a glimpse of my own reflection in the full-length mirror and barely recognized the man I saw, I knew I was exactly where I needed to be.

SOME TIME LATER, Dr. Garramone entered, appearing just as he did in his photo online: pristine hair, perfectly manicured goatee, and impeccable skin. A quick and precise handshake left a firm impression of confidence. His swift speech and fluid conversation made the meeting casual and subsided what anxiety was competing with genuine excitement for my future.

After talking about the procedural methods he would take, he turned to a more serious note. "So now let's talk about your shoulder and the dystonia."

Already struggling to process everything my still recovering brain was taking in, I tried to pay extra attention to the words before a couple handfuls pounded me in the head.

"I don't want you moving that shoulder much, okay?" he said.

Moving. Movement. So important to my dystonia. I *have* to be able to move. If I can't, I'm miserable.

"I need to be able to move it, though," I blurted. "If I—"

"You're right, which is why—now don't tell the other guys this—but you can do some gentle range-of-motion exercises, okay? But nothing strenuous." He proceeded to demonstrate a few light shoulder shrugs and shoulder circles. He explained that he usually advises no movement at all but in my case it would be a necessity. I had to go easy or else risk undoing the sutures or stretching the graft that would be my nipple: reshaped, repositioned, and reapplied.

"It'll be a delicate recovery, but I'm confident we can get good results."

Words kept rolling off his tongue as he addressed one topic after the next. He'd clearly been through this laundry list of items to be discussed with patients many times. But even so, my case was somewhat unique. He brought the conversation to the topic of pain relief and my addiction history.

"I doubt I'll take them as prescribed," I said. "When added on my usual meds, that's just too much."

Indeed, in the six months of full-time work plus part-time work, I'd began taking my heavy-duty neuro meds more closely to the prescribed levels. Adding on a narcotic could be a bad idea, given my consistently low heart rate and blood pressure.

118 — Nate Cannon

He offered his approval for my self-moderation. "You may want them, just in case. I'll give you the usual amount I give guys but cut the refills." I wasn't sure I'd ever even get through the number he counted. But then again, I didn't know what sort of pain I was about to get myself into.

We finished up, having agreed on the surgical plan, and I hopped back on the trans van. I left the appointment with only a prescription for Vicodin and presurgical instructions, ready for an early night filled with one last jog in a bra, one last night smooshing boobs as I contorted to get comfortable in bed.

One final night as a biological woman. One last shower in the morning, before heading off to surgery.

THE WATER DRIPPED from my body like fresh rain, crashing with a pop as each drop shattered, born with a splash. Nothing had been special about my own birth, but something must've gone quite wrong for me to have been born with these two overgrown and increasingly droopy lumps on my chest. These incredibly female attributes. The reason behind my own internal dispute.

This was the last shower I'd ever take with them. The last time I'd ever feel warm water run over them. Or push them up to wash under them.

This was the last time I'd towel myself off and do the postshower towel shake, feel them flap and slap against my skin. The last time I'd cover up in front of the mirror and wish them away. But for the first time in a long time, for a moment, I wished them to stay.

When the mirror cleared, their shape, feel, contour felt familiar. As if I were cradling the essence of my adolescence, the gift born on me, but the same gift that I had been willing to die to make disappear. I put my still soft, smooth hands up to cup the perfect petite handfuls, thumbs slowly caressing the minute crevices and contours of the outer edges. Under an inch each in diameter, each nipple. The peaks and valleys encircling the center grew firmer as the lavender-scented postshower scent dissipated and the temperature dropped. The centerpieces, so precisely circular, swelled outward, erupting as mountains sprung from the rocky ridges of the Earth's outer crust. A shift was in process.

The terrain was about to change.

This was my body. My shell. Parts I'd let those I'd loved kiss and caress as they pressed themselves tightly to my chest. The memories, I told myself, would never fade. Even if the flesh itself were to be taken away.

Each crevice and bump lining the pinkish-hued Mars-like surface of each nipple seeped into the pores of my fingerprints and dripped into my memory. I stood heavily, drenched by the reality that in just a few hours, these objects of my own disdain and of others' desire would be plucked from my body like a stray white hair on an otherwise youthful figure, sliced from my chest with precision.

Me? Sewn back up, the flaps of skin from the circular nipples grafted back onto a flat ribcage, placed precisely where a man's nipples should sit. The suture line running like a train track, tracing from the center of my breastbone, disappearing under my arms to leave behind merely a faint echo of my body's history.

The flesh? Placed delicately into jars. Sometime later, lab techs and doctors with white coats would remove from the jars the essence of my adolescence and nature's great mistake. They'd place them on a shiny silver surface similar to where bodies are deposited with toe tags. But my tissue, my flesh would come with no face and no name.

The terrain was about to change.

No more would these lumps of flesh be stuck to my ribs like self-perceived suspicious masses, thwarting my every effort at being seen as the man I was. No longer would they call out my gender and announce to the world my anatomy, leading the march or guiding my way. No longer would they lead the parade, pointing me to my intended direction. A bodily compass that lost its true north.

The terrain was about to change. My name, my face, my body, headed the same way.

I KNEW ENOUGH to know surgery wouldn't be painless. I'd read enough to understand what would be done. But no matter how prepared and ready you are, you never know what might happen when it comes to medical procedures.

The surgery is formally called a double mastectomy with chest reconstruction. I call it slicing off the tits.

These weren't parts I needed nor parts I desired to have. To the contrary, their very existence contributed to my decision to end my life nearly a year earlier. That attempt cost me everything but what I set out to lose. Now I was ready to lose them for good.

The outpatient surgical clinic was much further than Dr. Garramone's office, and each mile of the trip would have been far more enjoyable had I been able to run them instead of listening to the sorts of conversations I did. Drinking, sex, more drinking. It just wasn't my scene; I couldn't wear a mask any longer and pretend to be something I was not. Just as I was not a woman, I was not a drinker or a partier any longer. I was not an active addict; I was in recovery. I didn't care for sexual conquests; I was still trying to love my own self. Hungry as a wolf from the forced fast, I wanted no part of the conversation and slid my earbuds in to drift off into musical lullabies.

Upon arrival, the herd filed from the van into the waiting room of the modern and minimalist front lobby. A receptionist took my name and ID. She sent me back to billing, where I paid for the procedure. From there I was moved back to the front lobby, where I took a seat next to the others from my group. One by one they were called back. I waited. And waited. My patience grew thin. Tiny claws seemed to be grabbing, twisting my stomach from the inside, squeezing it raw. I shifted on the hard chair, thankful for having been given permission to take my meds, but eyeing longingly the water fountain as lips puckered and moistened beneath its arc. For what seemed to be an eternity, I waited. And waited. All the while watching others drink coffee and eat bananas and sit comfortably.

The biggest day of my life, something I was paying thousands for, and still I was grumpy.

Eventually I was called back, by my female name, for a blood draw. That led to a request to change into a gown. Which led to walking, socked and gowned, alongside a nurse, down a narrow hallway to a set of doors. Through those doors I was pointed to a bed.

Nobody came to introduce themselves for some time. Cold, hungry, thirsty, and increasingly uncomfortable, I struggled to find a position that would suit my brain's control over my body.

I elevated the head of the flat bed of the surgery prep room and thought I found that comfortable place. For a moment, I was still. Then my brain got up and darted through fields of unwelcomed yet nostalgic memories. The nights I spent as a young kid crying and begging my mom to let me be a boy, my devastation as a young adolescent when womanhood blossomed on my chest, being fooled by my sexuality as a young adult, feeling inconsolable when I reached an age where I could no longer call myself young. And devastated once more by the presence of breasts, my inability to just cut them off and make them disappear. Their existence was eating me alive.

The dysphoria tried to kill me. The breasts, far more so than what anatomy I had below the waist, were destroying my life. Finally I could get rid of them.

PERHAPS I SHOULD'VE told someone about my heart condition diagnosis. My failure to disclose that could have had deadly ramifications. I was lying on the gurney in a same-day surgery clinic in Florida for a reason. I'd vowed not to die as a woman. Not to die as Jennifer Cannon.

The pre-op room buzzed with noise unseen. White clogs, blue scrubs, tennis shoes, and dress slacks scurried by underneath the privacy curtains enclosing me. Just me. And my thoughts. Racing ever faster, trying to outrun the memories. It wasn't working.

What if the anesthesia fucks with me the way it did during ECT? I'm trying to live here, not die. I risked and lost everything for this moment. Telling them could ruin everything. But not telling could cause complications. Why did this just get so complicated?

I reeled myself back in from the station in my brain where the trains were departing in every direction. My mom. How she felt when I called her the night before I flew down to the retreat. She later told me she felt she was saying good-bye to her daughter forever. That she was losing her daughter. My insides quivered at the thought of her sitting back home, grieving my loss while also worried sick that something would go wrong with the surgery.

As I lay on a hospital bed, hooked up to machines for the first time since the coma, discomfort overtook me. I was growing restless physically, my dystonia urging me to move. But the sorrow, grief, and mourning mixed with the absolute anguish of living with a mistake of nature complicated the pure joy and excitement of finally having made it to this moment.

It's what my heart wanted. It also wanted a safe surgery. That meant disclosing the condition up front. *Perhaps,* I reasoned, *it would turn out to be nothing.*

A SIGH ESCAPED me as I leaned back on the bed in my gown, lost inside my never-ending racing brain, staring up at the fluorescent lights.

The curtain squealed open. "He's on his way," a young nurse said, conveniently checking the IV only just before the doctor arrived. This anesthesiologist, I realized, probably knew nothing about the various complexities of my situation. He likely knew me as just another surgery patient to whom he would explain his role. Get consent. Do calculations. Ask questions. Standard procedure for any medical procedure, even a socially obscure one.

Wait a minute. He'd ask questions. Ten minutes later, a slender older doctor with a Florida tan did just that. "Have you ever had a reaction to anesthesia or any other medications?"

Medications? Geesh. That list could go on for pages, and I wanted to get to this surgery before reaching middle age, to become a man before an age where women would assume I was too old to keep it up, judging me on the penis I wouldn't have.

Reel it back in. The doctor is here. Now. To see you. For this. The biggest surgery of your life. First him, then the surgeon. Garramone. The man. The name in FTM top surgery. To get to him, I'll have to get through this guy.

One last hurdle. I'd done what I'd had to do up until that point to get cleared to be there: I withheld information about a heart condition that arose postcoma and that I had been advised to follow up on. I never did. I'd been too scared to lose the opportunity to finally have my body anatomically corrected. "I've had some bad reactions to stuff," I finally mumbled to the doctor, patiently awaiting my response. "Mostly medications."

"What kind?"

"Anti-depressants. And anti-epileptics."

I knew the next question.

"Do you have epilepsy?"

Spot on. "No, but I've had seizures in the past. I have EEG abnormalities that look like epilepsy, but it's actually brain damage."

I subtly slid in the story of how a doctor of physical medicine recommended a facet joint injection to help my neck pain and gave me general anesthesia. During that procedure, my blood pressure or pulse dropped.

Then the rest of my history poured out as he questioned me. That reaction to anesthesia, the prolonging of the QT interval while under anesthesia years later for ECT treatment, the suggestion to follow up with a cardiologist and recommendation to stay away from a drug called Zofran.

Zofran is commonly used along with anesthesia to prevent postoperative nausea and vomiting. But it also can prolong the interval between the Q and the T waves of the heart, which had already become abnormally prolonged following my suicide attempt. All I'd have to do is endure a little vomiting and nausea to get through this then. All we'd have to do is just avoid Zofran, right?

Not exactly.

"We'll need to get a baseline EKG," the doctor said. "To make sure we're not overlooking anything."

A friendly, smooth conversationalist, the tan Florida doctor stood up from the chair at the bedside and exited the privacy curtain fortress. A woman soon entered, with what looked like a tiny computer from the '80s: a boxy white machine with a black screen showing green readings. She attached wires to my chest, soft glue gummed to the very flesh I wished to disappear. We made small talk until the results she couldn't tell me about arrived, straight out of the machine itself.

"Okay, I'll go give this to the doctor." She smiled and left behind a cloud of tension.

The sense that the results were going to be far too abnormal to proceed with surgery drilled a hole through my very well-being. The curtain directly in front of me swung open with a rush, bottom brushing to and fro on the linoleum long after it'd come to a stop. Florida tan man reentered.

"Well, this won't do," he said. "Let's get another one done. Where were you hospitalized?"

I relayed the information despite my internal hesitation. "Why?" I asked.

"I'd like to get those EKG records to see what they found."

I don't recall if I became emotional. Can't remember if I got mad. I have no memory of signing a consent form. But in the prep room I waited, tucked away behind the privacy curtain, my stomach panged by the forced fasting and stress of the uncertainty.

I'd taken on a $10,000 loan and risked my career, my family, and my friends for this. Was this opportunity really going to be just a pipe dream because my health wouldn't allow me to move forward? As I lay on the pre-op table?

My anxiety stewed beneath my skin.

Florida tan man flung the curtain open once more. "We haven't received a response yet. I'd like to just go ahead and run another test."

"And will I be charged for that?"

"No. You won't. We'll just keep running it if we need to. The first was moderately abnormal, the second less so. I'd like to see if we can get one that is just mildly abnormal."

The knife already twisting my stomach turned a little deeper. I thought doctors were supposed to help people, not make them feel worse. Before testosterone, I would've cried, but I was losing touch with my emotional side.

I shed no tears. Instead panic clenched me.

"Are you saying I can't have this surgery because I have a stupid heart condition that has never posed me any problems?"

"Not necessarily." He shifted his weight and cleared his throat. "We'll just run a few more and do it until we get one that's a little closer to normal."

That could take all day. "What if you don't get a normal one before it's time for me to go into surgery?"

He assured me that we'd get it done. That reassurance was much needed, my heart teetering on the verge of breaking into pieces that would no doubt necessitate reassembly or resuscitation. I wasn't going through that again. But this had the power to absolutely crush me, heart and soul.

Tan man exited through the curtains that were starting to remind me more of a stage at a play. Who would appear next? Turns out it would be Dr. Garramone himself. I hadn't disclosed the long QT syndrome. Now here he was, standing before me with his blue scrubs and bronzed skin. He was ready for surgery.

I guess my heart wasn't.

"I understand we're waiting on some EKG results, but I'd like to go ahead and mark your chest with this blue marker to pinpoint where I'll be making the incisions."

An unusual request, I suppose. It's like: *Here, lie back so I can draw on your tits.* It turned out to feel like a creepy game of Operation.

I pushed myself up on the bed as he instructed. He had an air of authoritative confidence emanating from his very essence, and I felt comfortable trusting his professional opinion regarding how best to align me for surgery. Certainly the way the dystonia impacts my posture had to be factored in. As did my dystonic shoulders and the structural damage on the right one. I was still working full-time and part-time while running marathons, but the nuances of my body and its unique chemistry needed to be taken into consideration.

He lowered the back of the hospital bed so I was lying flat. It was not as comfortable as I was hoping on the dystonia in my neck. Once I was flat, he gave more concrete and direction instructions.

"Lie as straight as you can. So everything is in line."

What I thought was straight was apparently not. He moved my shoulders and then tilted my pelvis. "There. Now I'm gonna do this differently with you. I might have your right arm a little further out to the side." He pulled a marker from his pocket and grabbed hold of my right arm. With delicate precision, he moved it a few inches to the right, as if doing intricate interior design on the exterior of my body.

"Alright." He pulled the cap from the marker. "Don't move, okay? This might feel a little weird."

The soft felt tip of the marker sank into my skin. I tried not to look but couldn't help it. A tall man in blue scrubs wielding a small object was standing over me while I was shirtless. Time seemed to slow down as the marker pressed into my flesh; each painstaking line he drew dragged on through his slow precision. It was reminiscent of a horror story of torture. It was extremely uncomfortable, with my brain trying hard not to think of the marker as a scalpel or, worse, another variety of sharp knife being wielded by a madman Garramone imposter. At the same time my irrational fears peaked, I fought the urge to giggle from the tickle of the marker against the flesh of my chest.

He moved on from the incision line for the mastectomy to the cuts for the nipple grafts. The unmistakable, nose-hair-twisting scent of permanent marker maxed my nasal tolerance. I couldn't hold still. I flinched.

"Sorry," I blurted, the doctor's focus visible through his furrowed brow and narrowed eyelids.

"It's fine. I'm almost done." Just a few more marks later he finished, stood back up, and recapped his pen. "Okay, you can put your gown back on now if you want." I did so as he discussed our next steps. We'd wait on the EKG report from my hospitalization and keep looking for a semi-normal EKG here and now.

The EKG woman entered stage left after Garramone exited stage right. Back with the machine. "Well, they're improving. But the QT is still a bit too prolonged for the anesthesiologist's comfort. We're gonna try again if that's okay." As if I'd say no.

Two or three more tests were run before she stopped. "I'll take these for him to review. Hopefully it won't be long now. I'll check on that fax again, too."

I was getting impatient. Hunger was eating at me, and I grow grumpy when my hunger level grows. With my testosterone levels recently having been increased, I was eating a lot. My anger was also more forceful. And my grumpy side came out even more easily when I was hungry and thirsty. These were not good things to mix.

I held it in. Somehow. I channeled it. I wrote.

> 10.11.12 11:11 am
> I'm starting to get uncomfortable in this bed, uncertain as
> to how this is all going to play out.

I just looked at the clock. It's 11:11 central. That time. That date. Everything that happened . . . maybe this time it will be my good luck charm, instead of the start of a downward spiral.

I'm tired of sitting here. I'm hungry. I'm tired. I'm cold. I just want to get in there and get this over. C'mon HCMC . . . I don't know why I didn't get these records before. I didn't want to mention this stupid condition. I didn't want to not be a suitable candidate. I fear now, after all I've been through to get here, that they may not be able to operate.

Just as soon as I typed "operate," the anesthesiologist entered the scene stage right. "We got it."

"The records?"

"No, we didn't get those. But we got an EKG that's close enough to normal to proceed. There's still a prolonged QT on it, but it's in the borderline normal range and that might be about as good as we're gonna get." He suggested I follow up upon my return to Minnesota, just as every other doctor who saw my EKGs had. "But before that, let's get you going with the surgery you're here for today."

A smile swept out much of the panic and fear that had been running frantic, crawling all over my insides.

"It's a big day for you!" the tan man added. "This is the beginning of a new life. I absolutely love working with Dr. Garramone's patients because I know we're doing something that truly benefits you. I hope this procedure helps you feel more at home in your body."

His words, his empathy, zapped what little anxiety and apprehension was left. He understood. And he had cleared me to go. Even the doctors knew this was precisely what I needed.

"I'll have the nurses come and get you," he added. "It won't be much longer now."

WITHIN WHAT FELT like hours but was probably only a few minutes, the entirety of my journey through dysphoria seemed to reel through my mind: from the moment I realized I'd never *wanted* breasts at all, but merely tolerated and eventually accepted them, to the fight to get approved for the loan that put me in the bed I was now lying in. My breasts were part of what society, and subsequently my own self, saw as markings of my feminine body. They were evidence of my femaleness, and they were finally ready to be properly disposed of.

The screech of the privacy curtain opening once more interrupted my reflective train of thought as two nurses came in and stood on both sides of the bed. "Ready?" one asked.

"It's been a long time coming," I said. "I'm more than ready. Let's do this."

They took the brakes off the wheels of the moveable bed and un-hooked the saline I'd been given via IV, hooking it to a post on the bed frame. They wheeled me through the pre-op room, past the nurse's station, and through a double set of doors.

The sterile silver, shiny interior suggested this was the operating room. As did the beaming overhead light. I reached up my hands and held my breasts in my hands one last time, knowing it would be the last time I'd ever touch them.

Memory starts to blur as the anesthetic cocktail began to take hold. Snapshot recollections of trays of surgical instruments moved bedside, a bright light, people with masks, instructions to not move, an oxygen mask. I drifted into semiconsciousness knowing that when I awoke, I would no longer need to wear any sort of mask.

14

Phantoms

What tissue didn't exist on my body until it developed against my wishes at twelve years of age was finally being taken away. Despite the sentimentality gripping my attention as the anesthesia from the surgery wore off, the excitement of finally being rid of them was also tinged with rage. Dr. Thorp had confirmed my hormone levels were off just three weeks earlier, and they were likely still low. And for the first time since shock treatment, I was being exposed to anesthesia.

The darkness stopped. The silence faded. Every subtle sound suddenly drilled through my ears, wailing screeches of carts as they went by, voices in the hallway outside. Outside what? I opened my eyes. Privacy curtains encircled me once again.

A woman with tan, lizard-like skin sat to my right in a chair, which I could tell even by looking at would bring on painful spasms if I sat in it. "Well, good morning, sleepy head," she said, sitting comfortably. "Ready to go? They've been trying to rouse you for an hour now."

What nice words to awaken to, especially coming from Karen, hostess of the retreat and surgery escort for the day. My stomach growled, matching the ferocity of my inner hormonal beast, snarling, frothing, at attention. Shivering pain snaked through me as I lifted the blankets to sit up and examine what contraptions I was still attached to. As I did, my inner Hulk turned green, bursting through my gown; the joy of my life-changing moment glowed with rage. Hunger. Pain. Cold. The perfect trifecta to tip the scales of my emotional balance. The wrong moment for the nurse to enter.

Her arched brows reflected the concern painted on her stare. My anger was visible, sweating out of my pores and soaking those around me, from the nurse to my own host. I have no idea why I was so pissed off. All I know is that I had just one very specific request: food and fluids.

"No," the nurse and my host echoed in unison.

I grew angrier.

"Listen to me," I leaned forward as if to amplify the importance of the forthcoming statement, "I know my body." Half propped up in the bed, fists clenching the sheets, it was all I could do to not raise my voice. It turned out to be a futile effort. Their silence only upset me more. "I need potassium!" I shouted. "A banana. Orange juice. Something!" These are things generally not to be consumed immediately after anesthesia.

Hunger and thirst and cold would only make me angrier, though, so I demanded food, trusting my body and the knowledge it had acquired through eight years of sobriety and six years of living with a progressive neurological disorder. A rusty metallic drip lingered with every swallow, singed every nasal inhale. The aftertaste of intubation only added to my restlessness.

I tossed my head back against the bed and let out a sigh, Karen still seated next to me. "If they'd just fucking listen to me, I wouldn't be so fucking pissy." As I cursed like a sailor, my anger drifted further from my control. The nurse reentered; I'd barely even noticed she'd left.

She'd folded. "Here," she said, offering up a small glass of apple juice and a duo pack of graham crackers. "This should tide you over."

"Tide me over? This? I don't think so. I'm a growing boy here."

The nurse smirked and shook her head.

Karen uncrossed her leg with a dangling, swinging sandal and plopped her hands to her lap. "What exactly do you want, Nate? I'll go get it. I agree that two graham crackers aren't going to tide you over, and clearly you know your body best."

Somewhat stunned by her sudden understanding, I hesitated as I formed the words. "Why, thank you," I said. "I just want a banana. Maybe cottage cheese or yogurt."

Though she didn't recommend dairy, fruit would be okay. I agreed. She started out of the room, leaving me to be alone for the first time since coming out of anesthesia. Instead of having any sense of how important of a moment it was in my life, all I could think about was food.

It was nothing new. In the weeks leading up to surgery, I'd started to develop hunger pangs to accompany my growing pains. I'd wake at 3 a.m., ravished with my stomach in tangles. My gut begged for food, jarring me awake. Cereal seemed a quick, simple, and logical choice. Milk has potassium, calcium, and protein, all of which I needed mightily. And the right cereal can pack a powerful nutritional punch.

What my brain knew as "full" before starting hormones had changed, though. Now I couldn't seem to satiate the beast of hunger. The signal from my brain got overpowered by my body's demands. I'd never craved meat before, either. But more and more, I found myself in a trancelike state, making my way through the grocery store with clear signals from my brain: *give me protein, must have meat. Feed me.*

While meat is a good protein choice, cereal was far quicker for my midnight pangs. Though I've never struggled with bulimia, I admit I did have nights where I later became so uncomfortably full that I forced myself to vomit. It seemed all I could think about, day and night, was food, often with a reduced ability to moderate intake. Or perhaps my stomach just needed to catch up to what my body truly needed. I'd grown to trust its instincts.

Evidently coming out of surgery was no exception to my hunger games. My body and brain kept nagging at me, imploring me to eat. There was a Nutri-Grain bar in my backpack, which was next to Karen's chair. If I could somehow manage to get to that bag, I could get that bar. Get those nutrients. But if I was gonna do it, I was gonna have to do it Bond style.

Examining the various tubes coming out of me, I discovered that, instead of being affixed to a bomb or some other explosive apparatus, I was hooked up to machines that would sound off with beeps if something became unattached. Stealthily I pivoted on my butt ninety degrees and stepped one toe to the ground. As I did, the pain squeezed my ribcage in a vise. I sat up straight from an already propped position and drew in a breath, but the air in my lungs seemed to drift upwards, escaping through my nose and ears like a balloon deflating.

Growing more light-headed, I realized this whole getting-up-before-eating-anything idea wasn't smart. I abandoned the mission, pivoted my butt back the same ninety degrees it came from, and let my head crash softly back onto the pillow sans bar.

By the time Karen returned a short while later, I'd already drifted back asleep. "A banana and a fruit salad," she declared, popping the top off a plastic box. The sweet aroma of fresh pineapple put me in a much better mood, and I quickly devoured everything. Still I was hungry.

"Can I have the Nutri-Grain bar in my backpack?" The words blurted out of me, straight from my stomach. It truly was talking.

Karen waffled before consulting with the nurse. I was given the green light. Since I was parched from the anesthesia and intubation, the soft grains proved more difficult to chew and swallow than the fruit had. But with water, I wrestled it down into the growling beast that had become my belly.

Most importantly, though, I got the banana I'd been craving, each potassium-loaded bite refueling the electrolytes I'd had to learn how to control through diet in sobriety. Much the way my brain was calling me to eat meat, dairy, and other protein-laden items while I was on T, it commanded me to eat bananas early in sobriety. I had never liked bananas, but I started to eat them and discovered that I flat out felt better when I did. They became part of my daily diet. It was also the life-preserving electrolytes that failed to reregulate themselves following my suicide attempt. As a long distance runner, I've learned how to replenish my electrolytes. I could tell they were off the moment I came to consciousness after surgery.

It may be hard for health care professionals to believe, but sometimes people truly do know their own bodies best.

FOGGY-BRAINED BUT ONCE again electrolyte-balanced, I was allowed to get unhooked from all gadgets and detached from all wires, standing up without lightheadedness to get myself dressed with assistance. Putting on a shirt wasn't going to be easy. For the next five weeks, I wouldn't be allowed to lift my arms above shoulder level. Button-ups and zip-up hoodies would fast become my friends.

Once dressed, I followed Karen and shuffled my freshly fueled frame to a van, where I reclined the front seat. Two other guys who had gone through surgery sat in the seats behind me, their British and Australian accents diverging and separating yet merging and coexisting. My heavy lashes began to close once more as our driver pressed her sandal to the pedal.

Behind me in the seats, phantoms of the person I wish I could be: Aiden, a Brit pub lover with a devoted girlfriend, and Ian, a rugby fan from Sydney engaged to a beautiful environmentalist. Social, neurologically normal, no mental health problems: they were celebrating a milestone in their own lives with people who loved and accepted them. I was still grieving the loss of the person who swore she'd be by my side at this moment in my life.

No drug in the world could take that pain away. But did that mean I didn't have anyone in my life who supported or loved me enough to accompany me to the surgery? Not necessarily. I still had people who cared about me, and new people were coming into my life right and left. But so many of my old friendships were changing or falling away. So, too, was much of my family.

I thought of my mom. How she must have been mourning the death of her youngest daughter. What was, for me, one of the most important days of my life was, to her, the day I truly died.

Loneliness drowned out the laughter behind me as I struggled just to get comfortable. Fighting the torque of muscles controlling me like a puppet on a string, and once again not feeling up to trying to socialize with the other guys, I let the meds take hold and closed my eyes.

When I awoke, we were back at the ranch. I immediately retreated to my room, away from the others. The combination of the surgery meds, which included Demerol, with my usual meds, plus Vicodin to boot, was taking its toll on my body. Sleep would not be a choice but a mandate. First, I needed to eat again. Karen graciously brought a bowl of warm soup, knowing I was the only guy there by myself and, apparently, quite an eater. The healing broth opened my sinuses as I lifted the first spoonful to my mouth. After just half a bowl, though, I set it aside, tipped the recliner back, and tried to keep the increasing nausea at bay long enough to drift off to sleep.

As I shifted on the seat, the bandage around my chest and mid-section shifted slightly with it. A subtle brush of my still hairless chest against the beige fabric of the compressed wrap. My skin. Against the bandage. Enhancing my awareness of my own sensory information.

Reality hit: my chest felt different. I couldn't see beneath the bandages or feel much beneath them. The lingering anesthetic would dissipate and fade, but the nerves that were severed and sliced would take months to heal. Until then, I would have very minimal sensation to touch. I didn't need to touch or see it to know that my chest *felt* different, though.

It felt flat. Which felt surreal.

I reached up and with fingers outstretched put both hands up to my chest. My fingertips danced like ballerinas along the tender, almost sticky surface of the wrap holding my newly grafted nipples into place. The wrap served also to prevent the overstretching of skin, ensure the suture lines from the mastectomies were covered and compressed, and assist with the management of fluid collection.

My fingertips served to remind me that the brain and body are intrinsically linked. Flat. Gone. My brain knew they were missing. But it also knew they never belonged.

THE FIRST FORTY-EIGHT hours proved to be painful. Despite being in Florida, I was to avoid direct sun. That, in and of itself, is a challenge for me. Sunshine lures me, beckons me to bask in it. Instead of going shirtless by the pool just yet, though, I'd be sporting a very attractive, tightly fitted six-inch-wide wrap compressed to my chest for the next two weeks. Interwoven between the dressing and the wrap were two clear plastic tubes called drains, flexible as straws with a similar diameter. The tubes emerged from the wrap near the nipple areas and were attached to oval shaped containers that looked more like travel-size shampoo bottles. The two bottles dangled in front of me as bait would on a fishing lure, clipped to the outside of the bandage to support the weight of the collecting fluid.

Every four to five hours, I emptied the containers and recorded for the doctor how much bloodied, serous fluid was oozing from the space

once occupied by my breast tissue. Triggered by the inability to manip-
ulate the positioning of the fabric against my skin, my dystonia flared,
contributing to my already pronounced desire to be left alone.

The other guys, who came from all over the world, from Australia
to New York City, seemed different. First and foremost, they all had
partners. They all seemed to be able-bodied and free of chronic illness,
though I could certainly be mistaken. They were often celebratory before the surgery, which we did share in common, but unlike me they
were celebrating with alcohol, both before and after surgery. Add on
some Vicodin and the early stages of hormone therapy for many of the
same guys, and the end result is a steady dose of energy with explosive
potential.

In other words, the house was full of unsteady levels of testosterone,
and I wanted nothing to do with it. I stuck to myself. I went for walks
in the sun, down the street to a small park. I sat out back alone by the
pool and dangled my toes in the water when the boys ran off with the
hosts to go to the mall or whatever trips they took. I was content to simply have some time not working. But more importantly, I was taking
time to simply be.

EVER SINCE THE coma and subsequent breakup, which was still less
than a year in the past, I'd been in "go" mode. Searching desperately for
work and then working seven days a week. Preparing the house for sale
and then selling the house. Facing the blatant discrimination of health
plan policies that deemed gender reassignment "cosmetic" and being
forced into taking out a loan. Jumping through health care hoops and
clawing through appointment after appointment. Losing my friends,
my partner, some of my family, and many of my supporters, all in the
very hopes that I would eventually find myself . . . exactly where I was.

On day three of my recovery, a trip to the mall was being arranged.
I elected to stay back. Bandaged, bound, and carrying drains around, I
didn't feel much like being out in public or shopping. I didn't even feel
like a man quite yet. Indeed, with my level of testosterone, my gender
could have been interpreted either way. And it was. I got stared at a lot.
It seemed people were trying to figure out whether I was a man or a

136 — Nate Cannon

woman, ascribe a label, and put me in a box. Or maybe it was all in my head, and that's just what I assumed they were thinking.

Regardless of my in-between status and my growing reputation for being the introverted loner at the retreat, I was happy to have time alone in the Florida sun. Even if I did have to keep a shirt on.

The humidity thickened the already boggy air as I slid the glass door shut and walked out to the pool area to relax in peace and quiet after the crew headed off to the mall. My senses opened to the tranquility of the moment with the silence left in their wake. The bright blue sky and giant clementine sunshine reflected brilliant designs on the pool's subtly rippling waters. Still a bit high on Vicodin and not enjoying any minute of it, I steadied my footing as I walked closer to the pool to sit on a claw-foot bench slab, as intricately designed and carved as the fountain directly across from me, on the opposite side of the pool.

I sat down and looked at the gentle ripples, the sun's rays shimmering and dancing along the surface. Each splash of water from the fountain traced reflective patterns as unique as snowflakes in flashes as quick as lightning from the shallow end to the deep end. The reflections in the shallow end, where I sat, and the shadows in the deep end became mesmerizing.

While I was in a daze, the sun moved from its position, causing what was a small reflection of my shadow on the water to grow ominously larger in size. Instead of creating a shapeless blob, it formed a human figure, genderless in appearance.

I looked down at the water once more, staring at my own shapeless reflection. I was still legally a woman, but with anatomy that would give me an affidavit to tell the court I was now medically a man and that my legal name, gender marker, and all legal documents should be changed to reflect that fact. Three months on testosterone is just enough time to have the Adam's apple begin to develop and the voice start to drop, just enough to have the shoulders broaden and the hips narrow, just enough time for the jaw to start to square up, just enough time for the questionability of one's gender to be most pronounced.

Man or woman, I could pass for either. But when people aren't sure what box you fit in, they'll create a box for you. It was an uncomfortable position.

In the gaze of my own reflection, I saw only the silhouette of a human looking back at me. A human being searching to find closure to the past, but with toes dangling into the waters of the future, mesmerized by the ambiguity of the present.

In that moment, I pulled out my phone and snapped a photo. It captures exactly what I hoped: the shadow of a shapeless, genderless figure whose reflection was staring right back at me.

I appear contemplative with my elbows on my knees. To my left a background shadow steps downward like a staircase. It then goes flat. My shadow, a mere phantom of the woman I once believed I was, rests in the middle of that flat line.

15

Boxed In

After two painful weeks of being unable to thoroughly enjoy the Florida sun with my now very itchy compression wrap, I awoke ready for follow-up. It was time to get those bandages off.

Having been told to sleep with my head elevated, I leaned forward from the mountain of pillows resting behind me and pivoted my legs towards the floor. As I stood, a nearly oily liquid started to ooze down my leg. With one more movement, the rest of the serous fluid spilled from the drain and splashed down my compression wrap, soaking the front of my pajama pants.

The day wasn't off to a good start. It could only get better.

In the trans van we arrived back at Garramone's main office, where we all filed out once more, some for pre-op appointments, others for follow-ups. Once more, the wait seemed excruciating, perhaps more so than the surgery and postsurgery pain combined. I'd been waiting for this moment all my life.

After tapping my foot nervously through the waiting room time, I found myself once again alone in a surgical-type room, with instruments on the table. One wall was composed of a mirror, while what looked like a dentist's chair sat in the corner opposite of where I entered. The instruments, and the bandages surrounding them, beckoned my attention yet again, before I remembered I'd wanted to videotape the moment.

Just as I got the camera set to roll, the door was flung open with confidence, a sure sign of Dr. Garramone's entrance. Quick and smooth discussion ensued before we got down to business. He explained he'd have to unwrap the bandages somewhat slowly to preserve the drains until he could get at them to remove them. He then described how to manage things going forward.

"I think you're going to be pleased with the results," he added.

The fluorescent lights, mirrors, and glossy marble felt less sterile and yet brighter than they had before, perhaps to provide adequate lighting for what many in the trans community have called the "reveal," when you finally get to see the results of the surgery.

Painstakingly, I held my arms slightly out to my sides, flaring the dystonia in my neck almost instantaneously, as he and his Barbie-like assistant worked to undo the many layers encasing me like a mummy. It was a lengthy enough time frame for a full discussion of what we were going to dress up as for Halloween, which was fast approaching. He and his assistant chuckled with their descriptions. I faked along, thinking, *Finally, this Halloween, I can actually be me.*

Once far enough down in the layers, the good doctor did something to release each drain. What that was, I could not see. But a few seconds later, he had a visual.

"Oh, that looks great. Fantastic. You're gonna like this." He stood from his kneeling position, not letting me in on the view yet, each second dragging on. Finally, with slow and suspense-fueled deliberation, most likely to ensure a suture didn't adhere to the gauze, he pulled away the final layer pressed to my skin.

I looked down.

They were gone. I couldn't believe my eyes. A smile collided with astonishment.

"C'mon over here and take a look in the mirror. I'm pleased with these results. This is good. As you can see, we have good symmetry here and . . ." he went on to explain how good of a job he'd done. He could brag all he wanted, as far as I was concerned. I was fixated on the visual before me. A flat chest. Yes, red. Yes, covered in stitches. Ugly by any measure of sexiness. But it was mine, and it felt as if I'd come home.

Just before I left the office, the receptionist handed me a folder with paperwork. In it were two copies of a certified affidavit attesting that I had undergone irreversible sex reassignment surgery and that my gender marker and legal documents should be changed to reflect that fact.

At long last, I could change my legal name and no longer have to be boxed in by an F.

JUST AS I began to feel at home in my own body, back home things weren't going so well. Brandi had texted me a few days earlier to let me know Ferrick wasn't eating. He'd been shuffled around so much, and so much had changed, his stress had to be through the roof. He was in yet another foreign environment without his usual parental companions. I'd written it off, or perhaps psychologically suppressed it.

Just after the marathon, and just before the trip to Florida, I'd found a lump on his side while petting him on the couch. I texted my sister, Chris, who had been a veterinarian. She couldn't say much without seeing him. But I remembered how he didn't react when I massaged the area, a move that any other time would've sent him launching from my lap. How his skin and fur felt matted, but not like a typical matting of cat fur—like a matted mass. I recalled investigating thoroughly the fine black fur of my then nine-year-old best feline friend, frantic in hoping my fingertips were deceiving me. The fear that followed when the hard, lumpy mass didn't move, had irregular borders, and proved not to be a knot of fur. How I feared he had cancer but worried I wouldn't have the money or time to be able to help him be comfortable. I remembered how that hurt.

That same hurt returned just as I returned to Minnesota, affidavit in hand. Thanks to Dr. Thorp's letter, I also had an affidavit from her as well as those two additional days off work beyond what I'd been told to take. It granted me additional time away from work—time to spend with Ferrick.

A few days after my return, I awoke with my usual hunger pangs and made my way to the kitchen before cold, wet chunks caused me to pull my foot up and flip on the nearby light. The projectile nature of the vomit decorating the kitchen cabinets seemed unnatural, the wet cat food coming back out completely and entirely undigested, hours after consumption. Alarm bells went off.

I'd been oblivious to his decline. I'd taken his presence for granted for so long and been so mixed up in work and other obligations that I was rarely home. I'd noticed before the sale of the house that he'd started to throw up more. I'd chalked it up to stress. This seemed far different.

I gathered the pet stain cleaner and a roll of paper towels, prompting Ferrick to leave his unusual place in the bathroom and walk past me to the bedroom. He went straight under the bed. Another red flag.

I left the cleaning materials behind and followed my friend, kneeling down delicately at the side of the bed, situated in the corner. After all, I was the only one getting in and out of it. Lifting the bed skirt, I couldn't even see Ferrick, his black fur blending into the unlit area. Bags and totes obstructed my view further. A glimmer of his eye caught the flashlight on my phone as I shined it to locate him. He was at the far back corner. He'd never gone back there before. And he refused to come out.

I texted my sister and asked for advice. She told me to bring him in as soon as possible. But there were barriers. It was daytime. I had relied on what few friends I had at the time for a lot lately. I couldn't burden them anymore, but I wasn't supposed to be lifting my arms above my shoulders or lifting more than five pounds. Ferrick weighed more than that, though as I spun for a solution, my brain recalled that he had lost weight.

Panic started to consume me as I realized I hadn't put the signs together. I called the closest vet, and they agreed: bring him in. I had no other choice. If I was going to save my cat, I'd have to defy my doctor's orders. Using my legs and forearms as much as possible, to avoid any strain on my chest, I pulled the weighty Tempur-Pedic bed and frame from the wall. Getting up on the bed on my knees, I inched along the covers. Just as I got to the corner, he got up to scamper and hide under the center of the bed.

Instinctively, I leaned forward and reached overhead with both arms to scoop him up, a stress searing through my chest wall as I did. Averaging eleven pounds during his life, he felt far lighter. I clung to him tightly and held him close. His yellow eyes engaged mine. The fear housed in his stare echoed what he surely saw in my own.

Though I remember little of the initial visit beyond the phrases "dramatic weight loss" and "tube feeding," I remember the words of the vet who looked in his eyes next: "He's sicker than I'm comfortable with."

I remember nothing of the first mention of cancer.

THE DIAGNOSIS CAME just as I settled back in at work at my scheduling job. The write-ups continued. The tension escalated on a daily basis. I had to get the hell out of there, and I was trying, even interviewing for a debt collection position, which would not have fueled my soul. But their insurance had already cost me an arm and a leg and $10k for two boobs. I had another round of Botox coming up and had more than reached my out-of-pocket max. If I could just hold on and hope they didn't fire me before November 1, I'd be happy. It would have made a lot of sense for them to terminate me on Halloween. It was the last day of the pay period and the last day of the month. It could have saved them some dollars.

Thankfully, they held off, firing me instead on November 2, with Erin even being so kind as to walk me through the building and all the way to my car. I lost my job, but I got to keep my lovely "gender reassignment is considered cosmetic" employer-based coverage one more month. That meant one more month without my psychologist. But one free round of Botox.

Everything is a trade-off.

NOT WISHING TO dwell on the situation, I started applying for positions in mental health and chemical dependency. Presenting as a man, in my first suit, I got hired on as a male tech at a three- to six-month inpatient program for adolescents with severe mental health conditions and chemical dependency issues. I was still legally a woman, though.

Scheduling court hearings can take time. As soon as I returned to Minnesota from Florida, I pieced together the documents to give to the court as part of my request for a name change. A name change hearing, in Minnesota, does not automatically equate to a name and gender marker hearing. In fact, it can be quite challenging for many transgender people to get their names and gender markers changed. A prior felony, for instance, could bar you. (Unfortunately, much as with suicide, transgender people continue to have disproportionately high rates of arrest and imprisonment.) I'd had a felony charge dropped after I was arrested at twenty while driving drunk.

Many trans people don't know that you need to specifically request a change in gender marker during a name change hearing. These folks may have a name change hearing go well, only to find their identifications are still showing the gender they were assigned at birth. But I knew how to work things and thanked my legal background for allowing me the savvy needed to navigate the court system. My hearing was set and pending when I started working with adolescents at a long-term inpatient program for mental health and chemical dependency. It would seem a long way off with how things got started.

The kids had seen me enter when I came in for the interview. By the time my first shift rolled around, my supervisor pulled me into an office to talk. A woman of my own height with spunk and a ponytail, she'd connected easily with me when we first met.

"I have some concerns," she said. I hadn't even started the job and somehow I was already in trouble. "The kids are talking."

I wasn't sure what to say but likely said much via facial expression alone. Though the grimacing, sighs, abrupt movements, odd postures, and slouching associated with my dystonia are often misread, my face still speaks on its own. I've been told I'm hard to read yet very expressive. "Intense" is often used to describe me. So was my brand-new boss saying the kids were already noticing this?

"They're talking about your gender. They don't know what to think."

Still unsure what to say, I started to think about my own self-perception and how others were seeing me. How she was seeing me, and how the kids were seeing me, was far different from how I was seeing myself. I was comfortable with how I was looking and presenting.

Yes, my gender was quite androgynous at the time, but Nate was coming to life. Despite that, my career seemed to be in limbo, in part because of how my gender—and my dystonia—were being interpreted by others.

My gender had been "confusing" to people with brain injuries and neurological conditions, of which I have both, and now it would be confusing to adolescents? I was one of those once, but it was then that

I'd lost conscious sight of my own gender. Perhaps out of my own discomfort. Maybe these kids were experiencing a similar discomfort, but not about their own gender—about mine.

I discussed the issue with my new boss. She reminded me that company policy prohibited me from disclosing anything about my chemical, mental, sexual, or physical health, and that my gender would fall in that category. I held my face in position so as not to show emotion. She went on to express how impressed she was that I was confident enough to endure what she worried was going to happen: harassment.

ON THAT SAME first day, I heard the whispers and felt the stares peering at me from behind. Both the boys and the girls seemed to wrestle with my identity, but in different ways. The girls seemed to see me as "gross." As the first night of my shadowing shift wound down, the kids were settling in for lights out. Armed with clipboards and walkie-talkies, a male colleague and I kept watch in the hallway while our third, female colleague did rounds through the girls' rooms. Everything was gender separated.

A slight squeak of sneakers against the linoleum floor was the only sound in the halls as our colleague closed one door gently before moving on to the next. As I looked in her direction, a door near me swung open. Out popped the head of a fourteen-year-old girl who had found her way to the facility all the way from the northernmost part of Minnesota. Her long hair swung out the doorway as just her face came into view. "My roommate wants to know if you had a sex change!" she blurted.

My colleague stepped in and advised her that her inquiry was inappropriate. I stood silent, somewhat in shock as to the word choice, but also keenly aware that I'd used those same words at age five. So, too, she was getting right to the heart of her curiosity.

It was clearly there. I'd already overheard her comment, "Eww, what the fuck is it?" and her under-the-breath statements of "faggot." That last phrase clued me in that she was not understanding the situation or what my identity was. As I had for so many years, she was confusing sexual orientation with gender identity. Just because I was transitioning to a man didn't mean I was suddenly attracted to men. I'd had a boyfriend in high school and still found myself noting men who were handsome, even dating Jeff from the psych ward. But I've always felt more comfortable with and attracted to women. My indifference to men was present when I was a woman. But more and more I was realizing that I had absolutely no desire to be intimate with a man as a man.

My new client made the assumption that I was an effeminate gay male. It appeared to me to be an opportunity for education, but policy prohibited it.

The boys were in a different role because I was hired as a male staff member. As a result, if they went out on a leave of absence with their parents and came back, it would be me whom they'd have to strip for. It would be me who'd have to take their pee. Me who would have to search their clothes, including their underwear.

This didn't go over too well with some of the boys. Some were uncomfortable having me in their room for chore and bed checks. Others refused to comply with strip searches. I had no choice but to respect their views, but at the same time, it did start to create problems. If I was the only male staff on duty and a male client did something that required a search or a urinary analysis, I had to do it. If they were uncomfortable with that, then they'd have to stay by my side for the rest of the shift. For the kids, this was a hard decision. But invariably, the boys stuck to their views and chose to stay by my side.

I didn't mind. I tried to use that time to build a bond and establish trust. But over time the weight of going into an environment where I was facing gender-based scrutiny from teens again grew heavy. Still, I'd come a long way. In these kids, both the boys and the girls, I saw bits of myself. Broken homes. School troubles. Mental health challenges. It was a looking glass into my child self, in a gender-segregated environment.

I used to be that girl spouting off to the counselor. I used to be that boy cursing one more time than his peer, just to one-up him.

The pushback the kids gave me stung. That is, until I realized that their discomfort was not about me—it was about them. And it was not rooted in any sort of fundamental hate or prejudice. It was simply discomfort from being around someone different from anyone they had known before. These kids had experienced traumatic events and done things many people are never exposed to or do. More than likely, they were open-minded. They just needed education. And to be in the know.

If the kids didn't know what was going on with me, how were they supposed to understand it? I challenged the management on the idea that gender identity is part of my sexual health. One of my colleague was mixed race. The kids would walk right up to her and ask: "Are you black?" She'd respond that she had one parent who was white, one who was black. "Oh," the kid would respond. End of discussion. End of gossip.

Sociological theory holds that race, class, gender, and sexual orientation are the four major frameworks that compose our social inequalities. Gender identity would seem to fall under the category of gender. This seemed no different from my colleague's situation. But in this instance, they were too scared to ask me outright or were told it was inappropriate to do so.

After the kids started asking the counselors during therapy about my gender, the tides shifted. Reluctantly but without a better option, the executive director approved my disclosure of my gender. Though I did worry about the kids' response, I was staying true to myself and becoming comfortable with accepting pushback while others worked on acceptance.

Most of my friends and family were struggling at the time, too. My mom resisted my transition at every step and seemed either unwilling or unable to use male pronouns or call me Nate. The more I'd demand she'd get things right, the further away she'd pull from me. It was an ongoing source of conflict between us until I realized that it was her struggle, not mine, to endure. I'd come to terms with my gender. Now it was everyone else's turn.

Unfortunately, that meant, in the case of my mom, not expecting that she get my name and pronouns right every single time. She'd been using female pronouns and the name she gave me for over thirty years. That's a tough pattern to break. Somewhere along the line I recognized I had to give her space. Excuse her. Let her grieve when she choked up after calling me Jen, knowing that person—the girl she birthed and raised—was not coming back.

Risking losing my intimate relationships, friends, jobs, and parental relationships is certainly not as risky as people not liking me because I offered them education. For my mom, that education would have to come in the form of visual change and professional growth. To recognize me as a man, she'd have to see it. She'd have to see the changes that were still questionable, even to the kids I was now working with. Back over at Gables, I was just Nate. No questions seemed to be asked other than by higher-functioning ladies sipping tea, commenting on what a kind and handsome young man I was. The residents all referred to me by male pronouns. There was no confusion, despite the fact that I was working with people whose condition caused confusion.

When it came time to break the news to the kids, though, I did so group by group, meaning gender by gender. To my shock, the boys gave me a round of applause. The girls offered nothing but supportive feedback, with a few, including the forthright sex change inquirer, shedding tears. Though that particular girl would go on to call me "faggot" countless more times and take shots at my gender when worked up, she also grew to trust me. She was just looking to strike me at the place she thought I was the most vulnerable, much the way I did when I was young, using and taking it out on counselors around me.

On her discharge, she requested permission to give me a hug. Any sort of contact was prohibited between the kids and the counselors. I agreed to it, and she immediately reached up and clung to me, reminding me that this human being with so much rage and struggle was still very much a child. "I'm sorry I said all those awful things I did," she said, as she pulled away. "You're actually a pretty cool guy."

Though I tried to stay stoic as I thanked her and wished her well, inside I wanted to cry, out of pure gratitude. Even though she hadn't been able to graduate successfully and had a lot of work to do on her own self, she'd grown. She'd learned a life lesson no textbook can teach. And she gained a perspective and insight into the human condition that will, I hope, be the groundwork for her own future recovery.

One client, then the next, thanked me for my authenticity. They didn't want a counselor who just went through the motions and kept emotions and personal life off the table. They didn't want a robot. I certainly wasn't going to stay in a role playing one, either. I kept feelers out for similar opportunities working with the LGBT community, as well as in California, as my court hearing finally arrived.

On 12/12/12, a date set by the court but that once more seemed to be a sign of numeric coincidences in my life, I returned to the same courthouse building where the courts had raked me over the coals about my disability just over a year earlier. So much had happened. I had been in a coma in a hospital less than a mile from where I now stood, postsurgery, on hormones, and ready to rid myself of Jennifer for good.

My brother John testified that I'd wanted to be a boy all my life. That this was right for me. The judge agreed. With a swift hearing and even quicker production of documentation, I left the courthouse in a far different mood from what I'd been in during my Social Security hearing. I carried with me a certified court document attesting that I should, heretofore, be legally known as Nathan Rhys Cannon. The judge also noted that all legal documents should be changed to a male gender marker.

Finally, I'd become a real boy.

Or at least, on one piece of paper. There was legwork to do now. First up: changing my driver's license. Next: my Social Security card. Then my passport. After that, I'd have enough documentation to change my birth certificate. That's a luxury as a trans person. Many states don't allow trans people to change that document.

In general, most transgender people do not have either the ability or the means to change all of these documents. Some people just don't want to. I wanted to change it all, whether I had the means or not. I never wanted to risk dying legally named Nathan, but having a birth certificate that still identified me as a female named Jennifer.

Having been born in Iowa, I was lucky enough to make the change. The new birth certificate took a few months to arrive. During that time, I changed everything else that requires changing, from energy bills to bank information to employer data to internet services. Each place seemed to have its own requirements, all of which were confusing. The energy company allowed me to change my name without much documentation at all, even though that's the document one would produce to prove residency. But changing my Comcast bill name proved a comedy.

After I explained the situation to one representative, she transferred me to her supervisor. Surely he would be more understanding, or something. Sadly, he seemed even more confused than the first rep. I tried to explain in different ways, but I didn't have a whiteboard to draw visuals to accompany what was apparently a very complicated situation.

I started to get feisty. He gave in. "Okay," he said. "But just so you understand, both Jennifer AND Nate will need to be present in person in order for this name change to be honored."

All I could do was laugh.

It seemed I was laughing more in general. Trying to get back out on the dating scene. Making occasional trips to see Heather in LA, where I'd easily made other new friends. My career seemed to be heading in the right direction, too. The work I was doing with adolescents offered solid experience on a résumé, complemented by what I was doing at Gables part-time. While I looked for LGBT-related opportunities in the Twin Cities, a job popped up with Gables in Santa Monica, home of the picturesque pier that represents the end of iconic Route 66. It was where Heather and I would often spend time.

It seemed the winds of change were calling me west.

I felt accepted in Los Angeles. There I could take my shirt off, play in the sand, and enjoy the sun. The city, the beach, from the moment my toes hit the sand, came to symbolize a boyhood I never had. Maybe this was just the change I needed. I applied for the position just as a job in an LGBT treatment facility in Minnesota came to my attention.

I applied for it, too. To my surprise, I was offered both.

I needed time to think about it. Too much was in the air. I struggled with the math, unsure what sort of wage increase would be needed in California to offset the inevitable health care costs associated with my neurological condition alone. Not to mention transgender health care services. I had an entire team of providers finally put into place in Minnesota, including doctors I'd seen for years. I was finally able to start seeing my therapist, Mindy, again as well. After stalling as long as I could, I accepted the position in California.

Something about the offer felt off, though. I couldn't risk getting out there and falling flat on my face: financially, emotionally, or physically.

Yet this was so perfect that it felt like a dream. I had to get to my Neverland. Reality kept calling, though, telling me this was not the right time. Not the right offer.

Eventually, I believed, that time would come.

So I ended up turning it down, but by that time I'd given notice on my apartment. I checked in with management, who'd been very kind about my transition, to see if staying in my unit would even be an option. It wouldn't. They'd already rented my unit out.

Minnesota in general had grown cold on me. I had no choice but to stay put, though. I put a deposit down on another unit across town, near the river, and rerouted my course once more.

16

Breaking Reality

"Sounds like you may be having what we might call a break from reality." My psychologist, Mindy, who'd been seeing me for four years, pushed her round-framed glasses up the bridge of her nose and leaned back slowly, as if to let me absorb the news without impact.

She'd never said those words before. *Break from reality. What exactly does that mean? That I pulled out my time card and punched out from life for awhile? Where'd I go?*

For some reason I imagined myself out driving a truck in the country on a bright, sunny day when a storm starts brewing on the horizon. I neither own a truck nor live in the country, but soon the clouds swirl closer, much as my thoughts race faster. The energy turns dark and heavy, surrounding me. I'm enclosed, encased, in a road race with a twister. Everything moves faster and faster as I press harder against the rain and debris, trying to outpace it, eyes shifting to and fro, from road to rearview mirror.

I search for something familiar in sight, but nothing is visible through the intensity of the rain, wipers dragging furiously across the windshield. The funnel of madness is gaining ground. I put the pedal to the floor. The faster I go, the less traction I have. Nothing is stable. The thumps inside my chest offset the heavy breaths, amplifying the internal noise.

In dead silence, all sound comes alive. It grates my ears such that the subtlest of droning hums begins drilling into my head, etching its way inside. A hollow echo overtakes my mental soundtrack. Unstoppable, inescapable, crashing against the banks of my psychiatric shore.

What would happen if I couldn't outpace it?

"LET'S JUST SLOW down here a second." My mental NASCAR screeched to a halt. I looked up. Mindy tilted her head slightly, a nonverbal communication often signaling sincerity, which psychological theory suggests lends itself to trust. "You're talking really fast, Nate. Let's take a few minutes, slow it down, and just breathe."

Just breathe.

Now there's something I hadn't thought of. I'd written at length about breathing in my first book: the role it played in my first suicide attempt at seventeen, how it's affected by dystonia and so crucial to the art of running, the fact that I was and still am breathing. But I'd ceased breathing since that first book came out, and I'd lost far more than I ever imagined when I came out. Despite the book's emerging success as a textbook and teaching tool, I still found it difficult to regularly employ the techniques I'd written about.

"Just breathe," I repeated to Mindy. "Just breathe. Yeah, I wish it was that easy. To practice what I preach. To just breathe . . . to just fucking sleep for that matter."

She stopped scribbling notes and perked up, at attention.

The insomnia had worsened in recent weeks, tossing my frame about the bed as I wrestled with adjusting to a rotating work schedule. My brain had clearly rebelled against the disruption to my sleep routine.

"Tell me more about how you're sleeping."

I'd been fighting nightly to quiet my racing brain, beating at my sanity, waking all too often entangled in sweaty sheets.

"New job, same story," I said. "They're discussing my health and are trying to drive me out, just like previous employers have done. They're having meetings about me. I know they are."

Another job now on the line, thanks to some stupid neurological condition that sounds more like an Eastern European country. I'd been here before. I didn't want to go through it again: the awkwardness of requesting accommodations, the subsequent pushback or mute response, the throwing around of legal terms like "undue hardship." I'd never had any trouble in a workplace until dystonia set in—even in the midst of active addiction when I was young. Now I was looking at yet another job where I was struggling to perform the duties assigned to me.

More importantly, though, I was growing alarmingly paranoid. Whom could I trust? Could I trust myself? Who the fuck was I?

Nothing was real anymore. My own reflection became unfamiliar. Not from the visible ambiguity of my gender due to where I was at in transition, but because of the very question of existence: *Was this really happening?* Was this moment in life, with the racing thoughts and the week or couple of weeks of minimal sleep to no sleep all a dream? I felt outside of myself. In vain I attempted to heed Mindy's suggestion: *just breathe.* But more and more it seemed that even when I slowed my pressured breaths in an effort to release the viselike squeeze on my brain, it didn't work. In the days leading up to the appointment, much the way I had when I'd wrestled with my gender dysphoria, I'd found myself staring hard in the mirror, straining to reach the soul of the person locked inside my eyes. The gaze of the stare looking back at me had become increasingly distant, almost lost.

With dysphoria, I felt out of place, and thought everyone was staring at me. But even in the throes of the darkest moments of those days when I questioned whether I was supposed to be Jennifer or some guy whose name I didn't yet know, I still knew I was *me.* I knew my identity. I questioned only if I was in the right body, if I knew my true gender. This time I wasn't questioning my gender. I'd flat out lost my grip on my own sense of self.

"Okay, well, there's the employment issue. My question was about your sleep, though. Are you sleeping at all right now?"

I didn't have an answer, but I did have a question. "What did you mean when you said I might be having a break from reality?"

She cleared her throat and sat back. "Well, sometimes when our thinking isn't grounded, we can lose sight of what's real and what's not." A momentary pause felt like an eternity before she continued. "It's also called a psychotic episode."

Psychotic? That meant crazy.

I looked up as the woman who'd cleaned up more of my verbal vomit than anyone but my mom softened her brow. Our eyes connected. I struggled to maintain the intensity.

"This seems to confirm that bipolar is the more accurate diagnosis for you," she said.

I released eye contact as the news hit me like a wet noodle at a pool. It's not surprising in that arena to be hit by a wet noodle because you're prepared. Still, you might be slightly stunned on impact. I was prepared for a bipolar diagnosis. It had been a possibility raised by providers since early in my college days. It seemed to explain things that a depression diagnosis did not. And quite frankly, it seemed to fit my symptoms.

Mindy went on to explain that she felt I was experiencing a "mixed episode," meaning I was experiencing both the depressive symptoms of major depression as well as the manic highs of bipolar at the same time. That made even more sense. But unlike in other forms of bipolar, the manic highs of mixed episodes aren't generally grandiose or even pleasant: they often involve extreme anger and paranoid delusions.

Finally, some twinge of emotion hit me. And it hit me hard. I leaned forward and put my elbows to my thighs, palms reaching up to massage tiny circles in my temples. A sigh escaped me, expelling with it what fragments of disconnected reality still remained. Breath by breath, I began to piece the world back together.

"This is one of the scariest things I've ever experienced in my life," I finally said. "I'm afraid I'm gonna end up losing my mind for good." Tears and rage stirred together to bring a salty flavor to my dry mouth. "That I'll end up in some group home or nursing home, forced onto anti-psychotics." I looked up, chin quivering. "I won't let that happen. They can't make me—they can't make me take an anti-psychotic. I know the law, and in Minnesota they can't make me without a Jarvis order, and we're a long way from that here, so I suggest we just . . ."

"Nate." She spoke assertively. It stopped me in my tracks. Years of respect building and trust that was well earned forced me to listen and not get defensive. To remember that I was absolutely terrified and this was the exact person I needed to ask for help from. Another reminder to come back into myself. To steady my breath. To *just breathe.*

"Nobody is forcing you to take anything, Nate."

My eyes were closed again, this time with a tissue pressed up against them, quivering shifting to the core of my body as I reeled in the emotion.

"My goal right now is to make sure you're safe."

To demonstrate that, I'd have to put on the performer hat and act as if I had my shit together, even if I didn't. After adopting the part and agreeing that I wouldn't go home and off myself or drink, I was free to go, thankfully not in handcuffs.

I returned home from the impromptu psychology appointment with a letter ordering me off of work for a week and also indicating that, due to my diagnosis of bipolar, I would no longer be able to work any sort of evening or night shifts. The change from day shifts to a rotating schedule is what threw off my sleep in the first place.

It was the first time my mental health directly interfered with a job, and I wasn't entirely stable yet. As soon as I left the appointment, I teetered on the verge of funneling back into madness, reality replaced by unfamiliarity with my own sense of person, time, and place.

Was I a real being? A ghost? Was this reality? Why did the papers say it was 2013 when it seemed like 1998? Was I really drinking coffee while driving on Highway 100 en route to a work meeting? Why did everything around me seem to be moving so fast and everything inside me seemed to be racing frantically just to keep up?

Unlike the exacting control I force into marathon running, there was no consistency; I was up and down and all over the place. Feeling infused by energy, I wanted to take on several projects all at once and accomplish them in an unreasonably short time frame. The ambitious desires grew more urgent, morphing into insomnia.

If I didn't either disappear entirely or accomplish my goal of getting to California and getting a master's degree, job, and living space—all by the end of the day—something very bad was going to happen to me. I'd lose the roof over my head and end up on the streets. Then I'd end up smoking crack and going on to sell my body and just keep using until I wound up dead.

I couldn't let that happen, even though, paradoxically, death was still very much an urgent need on my mind. All I wanted was to make it stop. To make the pain stop.

For good.

More pressingly, during psychosis, I just wanted to get off whatever fucking carnival ride I was on. If that meant death, so be it. Anything would be better than heading where I was going. The racing thoughts, ambitious in nature, intertwined and played off of fear and anxiety. That then spawned the paranoia and suspicion, accelerating the pace of the thoughts even more so. The paranoia heightened, and the suspicion increased. Angry energy dripped from my very aura. My chest heaved with anxiety as I tried not to let the magnetizing presence of insanity lure me any closer, but the pull was inescapable.

I lost more traction in reality. Why couldn't I turn the thoughts off? Why couldn't someone just kill me and make this stop before I did something really reckless like drive my car head on into another? Or frolic down Lake Street naked but for a beanie during rush hour in the January snow while singing "American Pie"? The latter would be far more likely, but the prospect of having no control over my actions while mixed in a simmering stew of paranoid psychosis scared me more by the minute.

The roller coaster kept getting faster. My brain kept revving up higher. Eventually something was gonna have to give. If I didn't stop this ride or get some help to get it to stop, I was not going to come out alive.

I kept in touch with my providers. Saw my psychiatrist. Saw Mindy again. Slept. I recall none of the time I apparently spent trying to get my shoes to once again stick to something called "reality" after the first psychotic psych visit.

At some point, though I hadn't physically gone anywhere, I found myself utterly exhausted. Colleagues and friends started telling me I'd been behaving strangely. Colleagues who doubled as friends mentioned I'd been acting more paranoid. Friends noticed me doing things out of character, like emailing at midnight. So where'd I go? Nobody knows. But perhaps I should put up a sign next time before I depart: *Gone Mad. May or May Not Be Back Soon!*

ONCE CLEARED TO return to work, I gave Nicha, my still-learning-the-ropes supervisor, Mindy's letter regarding shift work. A day later, she pulled me from my shift.

"HR is on the phone," she said sheepishly, handing over a note regarding my caller. "They need to talk to you right now."

It was the end of the road. The other shoe was about to drop.

I picked up the receiver to hear the nasally twanged voice of Patti, head of HR. Her tone conveyed unmistakable unfriendliness as she explained that she'd received the letter from my doctor.

"We have no choice but to put you on leave effective immediately," she said, sternly. "We'll call you to set up a meeting for next week to discuss next steps."

THE MEETING, WHICH was at corporate headquarters, proved to be no less tense than the call. Directed into an open conference room by hand signal, I looked out the open second-story windows to the vast flat lands of the snowy Minneapolis suburbs and walked around to take a seat on the far side of the table. We settled into an awkward silence. Me on one side. Them on the other. Such positioning is inherently adversarial.

I put up my walls. Guarded myself from inappropriate questioning.

"So," Patti began, "what do you think this meeting is about?"

"Well," I said, lump dropping from its place dangling in my throat, "I don't know exactly."

Patti kicked one open-toed flat over the other and pushed her chair back from the table ever so slightly, perhaps in an effort to loosen the atmospheric tension. "We simply want to talk," she said. My gut responded with a rush of distrust.

Nicha sat silent, tugging at her engagement ring and spinning it on her ring finger.

"Okay," I said. "I'm open to discussion. Where would you like to start?"

"Well, we got this letter from your doctor, Nathan." HR always seems to address you by your full legal name. "And had to remove you from the schedule."

"I don't understand. My offer letter states I was hired for first shift. That's what I agreed to, and that's part of why I accepted this position. I did not agree to be placed on rotation and was assured when hired that I would not be." I bit my lip, hoping it would somehow seal my tear ducts from any leakage.

Patti's eyes widened. "Yes, you were offered first shift. True." She cleared her throat and put both hands to the table as she leaned towards me, pen clinking against the wood tabletop.

"Your body is failing you, Nathan." She shook her head slowly, sloped brows and sad frown causing her droopy face to resemble a basset hound. "It's *failing you*."

Ouch. Low blow.

There had to be a way to work around this. I clung to what glimmers of hope I could retain as Patti posed one questionable question after the next. In the end, she agreed they had an obligation to try to accommodate me as an employee with a disability, or place me in another comparable role within the company.

"There are a few positions available for which you're qualified," she explained. She pushed a piece of paper at me and showed me the job titles. I agreed to interview for both positions we thought to be a decent fit. "If anything else comes up that you're qualified for, we'll let you know." Sure they would.

Another piece of paper slipped slowly beneath my eyes. "Lastly, before we go," Patti slid in, "this is the form that states that as of today, you are being placed on leave indefinitely."

Red flag. "Will I be paid for this leave?" I asked, one eyebrow creeping upwards.

"Yes, you will." Patti went on to quickly gloss over the most important points of what I needed to know. Only a fraction of the words reached me. Believing I was signing a form that would ensure I was paid until we figured out a solution, I put my freshly honed male signature on the dotted line.

Three weeks later the paid leave ended. I'd applied for jobs elsewhere but was assured interviews internally. They turned out to be fruitless endeavors. The company clearly had no interest in keeping me.

My economic picture once again switched on a dime, and once more my dystonia was also taking a stepwise progression. The falls while running had become more frequent, and the bend in my trunk became more pronounced. The lean to my right became more apparent. Comfort appeared like the contorted shape of a pretzel twist. Like the pretzel, I was salty. My anger grew thicker, more viscous, oozing through my veins and sticking to the capillaries.

"It's going to kill me," I'd often told my providers. "My circumstances are going to kill me." The concerned downward curve of the eyes coupled with the sloping of the brows keyed me into their concern.

The troubles started before the suicide attempt. But they amplified in the face of the coma and still very pressing gender disconnect. Sprinkle on testosterone, and I became explosive. But when the levels got evened out and things were stabilized, I no longer had an excuse for being so damned angry all the time. I don't mean a little irritable, like a grumpy grandpa when the morning paper hasn't been brought to the breakfast table. I mean rage-filled energy, the type commonly thought to be possessed by those who "snap" and end up shooting multitudes of people and, in the end, often themselves.

Much the way it feels while hanging, when the tracheal airflow squeezes to a halt and the blood begins to rush to the head, the anger becomes urgent. Pressing. I can understand the abuser's side of domestic violence. I've been there. I've been the alcoholic who hit my girlfriend. Was it any more excusable because I appeared to be a woman then? Or because I was drunk? I'm not sure. I'll never know the answer. But the guilt and shame of such behavior, such outbursts of anger, seemed to stalk me ever more relentlessly. After all, it was the factor that finally pushed Krissy away.

Regardless of whether it was the first suicide attempt at seventeen, the drug use, the concussions, the bipolar, the second suicide attempt, or the testosterone that followed all that, the fact is this: I struggle with managing my anger. The energy is palpable, radiating from my being, and it flat-out scares people. Honestly, it scares me, too.

It has cost me long-term relationships and long-time friendships; it has amplified my own self-loathing. It's pressed against my trachea and strangled my self-control with strength enough to force away all memory of the moments that followed, as the chemical imbalance pressed and swelled against my sanity.

The Hulk episode in the bathroom at work was merely the start of how testosterone would come to challenge me. I could blame the postanesthesia rage on those same imbalanced testosterone levels back a year earlier in Florida. But I had no excuse anymore other than the circumstances of life itself: simply *being* on testosterone, having a brain injury history, and apparently, also having mixed-episode bipolar disorder that had been wrongly diagnosed and treated as major depression for twenty-plus years.

17

Frozen

People told me I smiled more when I worked with the elderly and especially those living with memory loss. There was an awkward blessing for me in working with people who have dementia, too, because they often lose sight of gender. They may refer to even the prettiest, most openly feminine woman as a man and most masculine man as a woman. While that is, in fact, a serious symptom of the progression of the illness, it's also something that benefitted me.

I'd been working at Gables almost two years, since before my transition. The residents never noticed my gender change as it happened. Most referred to me as a man before I even felt comfortable being Nate on the job, months before I legally became a man. In my mind it felt as though they could see the real me, but of course, clinically it was more likely that they made the association because I had short hair and dressed as society collectively expects a man to dress. They certainly didn't know my name. Or know when it changed.

They weren't alone in how they were seeing me. How you and your brain interpret a person's gender by appearance (including hair, how they dress, mannerisms, and so on) happens in a split second. How we process all of that information and the conclusion we draw is often referred to as "reading" gender. Most people I was meeting, from cashiers to classmates, were reading me as a man. I was starting to be seen as a man in the everyday world, not just in the world of dementia.

Something curious was happening in the process, though. My true gender—my identity of being transgender—was becoming invisible.

Just like my disability. The bar was now raised: I would, from here forward, officially be seen as an able-bodied white man.

As a result, assumptions were starting to form. Numerous people at work asked me to fix the cable that went awry in a resident's room. Or look at the toilet that wasn't working right. I got asked more about my thoughts on football and began being recruited to help lift things I probably shouldn't be lifting. I played the role. Just like when I was a young girl playing hockey, I had to show I could hang with the boys.

I'D JOINED THE YMCA a few miles from my apartment, since my place didn't have a gym and I got a deep discount through my employer and health insurance. At my last apartment, which had its own pool, I'd discovered swimming the backstroke, the only stroke I could do with my dystonia and orthopedic issues, helped loosen my muscles. Just treading water proved beneficial for my dystonia.

But a pool in an apartment complex rarely frequented by others is far different from the world of the men's locker room. There were so many unwritten rules of behavior I didn't know. I also couldn't strut my junk, balls out, like the old timers seemed to do, proud and free. I couldn't shower nude like everyone else seemed to. I couldn't even feel comfortable changing, just as I hadn't previously felt comfortable changing in the women's room.

To make matters worse, a certain locker room regular had taken to hollering, "Hey, buddy," in my direction. I knew he was talking to me, but each time I'd just do that upwards nod that seems to symbolize acknowledgment and camaraderie, then look away and keep moving. One day I didn't have that choice. He walked right up to me. I stopped, looked up past a white towel tied under a drooping belly to the gap-toothed smile of a middle-aged redheaded man.

"Hey buddy. You sure you're in the right locker room?"

A cascade of images, of both personal history and of possible scenarios that may ensue, created a mental waterfall. My guard went up. *He must think I'm a woman in the men's locker room.*

"You old enough, ain't ya, buddy?" He scratched my head with his knuckle then walked away.

Moments like those would come to define my being. For myself, as for so many trans people, there is often a worry that your identity will be "found out" or seen as a threat somehow. This is particularly true in gender-divided areas like bathrooms and locker rooms.

Brandon Teena, a trans man who had not undergone hormone therapy or surgical correction, was raped and murdered on December 31, 1993, in Nebraska, after "friends" discovered he had a female body. That event came a year after my first diagnosis of what was then called gender identity disorder, just two hundred miles away, in a state that sat just across the interstate from where I was being raised.

Times may have changed. But hate is a powerful thing, and trans people are still at high risk of being victimized. The possibility of my being raped and killed has been, and probably always will be, my mom's biggest fear. And to this day I worry, when I walk into the men's room, enter a stall, and start peeing, about what others might be thinking as they hear that unmistakable pressurized sound pinging against the walls of the porcelain goddess while observing small shoes under a stall, feet pointed the wrong direction.

Despite the change in expectations and people's collective assumption at the time that I must be a boy of roughly eighteen years of age, I gained no additional skills as a man to add to my repertoire as my transition unfolded. Now, after over a year on hormones, I just looked like Brandon Teena—at least according to various people. In the workplace I looked too young for the job—and, evidently, now also for the men's locker room.

This was a whole different arena to navigate with my gender. Single-stall bathrooms would become a saving grace.

Even they couldn't protect me from having my scars seen or identity discovered in the pool area, though. Typically I frequented the Y early in the morning, around 5:30 a.m. On occasion it didn't pan out, or I wanted to swim after work to relieve the stress. One afternoon, waves disrupted the rhythm of my slow laps as I worked to wear out my overactive muscles. I turned at the end of the lap, eyeing a duo of rowdy twenty-somethings who had jumped in. They looked familiar.

My gut told me they weren't friendly. They knew me from the treatment center across the street, a facility that had housed the LGBT clients I worked with next to recently released inmates. I worked in that facility on a few occasions, right when I started, before the LGBT program moved to a building of its own. The place across the street brought their clients to the Y a couple times a week, but not usually at this hour. I wondered if maybe their schedule had changed.

Just as with the "Hey" man in the locker room, gut instinct told me I was unsafe. Thankfully I'd been wrong about him. These two didn't seem quite so benign. I planned my exit, but not before a thud and echo slammed against my head.

A tuning fork test of the emergency broadcast system rang in my ears as I struggled to get my bearings. I wiped the water from my stinging eyes and saw a water polo ball bobbing harmlessly before me.

Fight-or-flight response kicked in. There was no reason for the dodge ball they were horsing around with to be rifled in my direction from the deep end of the pool. It made no sense. There were only two of them. As I pondered, I could hear them start laughing.

I had to get out. My anger was starting to kick in. The T surely wouldn't help. This made for a bad mix. I didn't need a locker room fight to prove myself a man.

I tossed the ball back in as friendly a fashion as possible, unable to process any response while feeling some internal urge to either kick their asses or run away. I certainly wasn't going to be kicking their asses. I chose door number 2, exited the stairs on the shallow end, grabbed my towel, slipped on my sandals, and flip-flopped my way towards the showers. As I headed up the always slippery and precariously angled stairs to the locker room, two pairs of footsteps followed behind. It was them. I opened the doors. Through the steam I could see legs, signs of men raising their arms and scrubbing away. They wouldn't do anything with other men in the showers, right?

I rinsed. Tried to play cool. Pretended to possess no fear. Acted as if I didn't even notice they were there. But, like animals, they sensed it. They each took a shower on the opposite side of me and began talking to each other, seemingly eyeing me. Awkward and anxious, I closed my shoulders forward to hide my chest, fumbled the nozzles to the off position, and scurried to my locker to collect my things. Dexterity slowed by my haste, I fished the locker key from my swim trunks, fought with the locker keyhole, and eventually retrieved my clothes to scamper off to the private bathroom stall to change. Door locked.

I took a breath, heart thumping, and put my back to the door. How could I still my thoughts?

Eventually I'd have to return to my locker.

When I peered out, emerged, and started my trek, my two followers and their ink coverage stood waiting. Right next to my locker. With their cigarette scent and disheveled attire, I knew they *had* to be from the treatment center.

I approached cautiously but with certainty.

"Didn't mean anything by that ball, bro." I can't recall if I successfully avoided eye contact with the taller of the two, who seemed to be the instigator, and who was now initiating conversation.

"It's alright," I mumbled, packing my towel and wet swim clothes in a hurried and haphazard way I normally would never see as acceptable.

He leaned down and looked me in the eyes.

"What did you say?" He enunciated each word with intent. The lines that formed with his anger, greeting the scars and divots dotting his face, aged him significantly.

The fear within me felt manageable. For some reason, in times of intense crisis, I also tend to get more calm. I held his eye contact only briefly before looking away. If I just kept calm, practiced what I learned, I'd be okay. But crisis deescalation doesn't seem to work as well when it's you in the crisis.

"Oh, I just said it's alright, that's all. Don't worry about it, man." Friendly seemed the best avenue. He didn't read it that way.

"You gotta problem, bro?" He towered over me by a good foot but was kind enough to hunch forward to be closer to my level.

"No, there's no problem, man. I said it was alright. Just let it go." I threw my backpack over my shoulder, closed the locker, and turned towards the door, pace quickening. He shouted words I can't remember and probably wouldn't want to as the locker room door shut. I headed straight to the lobby where I caught the attention of the receptionist as I passed by.

"A guy, I think from the treatment center, just threw a ball at my head and then threatened me in the locker room." I can't recall if I explained I was trans. I was still getting used to the idea of telling strangers at that time. I simply wanted out of the building.

My fear didn't dissipate until I arrived back home. The next day at work, I told Nicha what happened. Her eyebrows, always so expressive, angled at the outsides of her eyeliner-lined eyes. She looked concerned. She'd spent a lot of time in that building.

She turned to the computer, pulled up a client's record from the treatment center and turned the monitor towards me, where I sat at the computer station next to her.

"This isn't one of the guys you saw, is it?"

I didn't have to examine the picture. I knew at first glance. "Yup. That's him."

She pulled the monitor back along with her lip. Momentary silence brought on millions of questions. Namely, *Why?*

"Well, your gut served you well," she said, adjusting the position of the stapler and other items on her desk ever so slightly. "He's a dangerous guy. He last did time for kidnapping his girlfriend and putting her in the trunk of his car," she turned to look at me, "and also has a history of crime against the LGBT community."

I'd wisely heeded my body's warning—but I hadn't recognized the depth of my risk.

I began to draw more and more into myself and more isolated from the world.

As I sat on the speckled beige carpet next to the bed with my cancer-riddled cat curled up in the crook of my bent leg, the cold Minnesota winter felt even colder on Valentine's Day. I stared into the closet, the one the ghosts told me to keep open at all times, with death on my mind. How could it not be?

The tumor on Ferrick's abdomen had continued to grow, swelling over time like a balloon hooked to a slowly dripping faucet. Rarely did he even enjoy the sunshine anymore. After he'd lived in the house for so long, moving apartment to apartment must've been taxing on him. I couldn't stand my current apartment, though. The creepy landlord who opened my door unannounced at 10 p.m. on a Friday night. Who asked invasive questions about my disability when I moved in. Who seemed to be watching me. That was enough.

The ghosts were watching me, too. The ones the neighbor told me about. They knew I knew they were there. I could feel their energy. They'd opened the closet, turned on the water, moved pictures, showed up as shadow figures in the hallway. Paranormal activity was not helping my mental health.

It seemed I was slipping away again, losing my mind and my way in life, unable to make it in any career thanks to an invisible disability that had been stripping me of my purpose with its progression for seven years. Learning through the grapevine that Krissy was already engaged to a woman—marriage equality becoming legal just a year after our separation—didn't help my outlook.

The suicidal thoughts became more pressing. What was holding me back? Third time's a charm, right? Nobody would find me this time.

YOU WAKE UP at an hour most consider the dead of the night but that you consider the heart of your soul. You'll listen to the steam crackling off the top of the coffee pot as it finishes its brew and see a still full bowl of cat food on the floor, cat nowhere near. He still doesn't want to eat, with the cancer eating at his abdomen, swelling at such a slow rate it only adds to the disguise. You won't see how distended it has become because you will have gotten used to it. Just as you will have gotten used to sipping your coffee at 3:47 in the morning, preparing to go out for a run.

You won't shed any tears as three beeps on the microwave announce the readiness of your lumpy oatmeal. You'll top off your coffee and begin preparing for another subzero run in one of the coldest winters Minnesota has ever seen. You'll wonder if your body will handle it today. If your will can sustain you much longer.

Yet you sit on a foot stool, outside a coat closet you've fashioned to be your running closet, and don your layers. You tie your shoes, put on the *ski mask, and contemplate your next move. But for your headlamp, you'd appear prepared to burgle.*

But you're no burglar. You're being recognized as a speaker and champion of mental wellness and chemical health. You're an author and being read by students who seem to idolize you. You're on a pedestal. You give and give through your work with chemical dependency, mental health conditions, and dementia. You no longer have room to struggle. You have your shit figured out.

So you'll brace against the wind as it singes your lungs into an icy pause of breath. You'll wait in the heated entranceway as your watch thinks about turning on and getting a signal in what the weather app reads as double-digit below-zero temps for the umpteenth day in a row. Your thoughts will slow as the deep freeze seeps through your layers, dipping into cold areas of scarcely visited emotions that drain you of your energy. You've been fighting so hard just to stay afloat. Each day seems to be getting a little harder. If you just keep on getting up and running, getting up and going to the gym, you'll be okay. You'll make it. "Make it where?" you'll wonder aloud, talking to yourself at what's now 4:20 in the morning. Years ago, you would've still been up at this hour.

Still awake.

Still drunk or still high on whatever, but with thoughts starting to lean towards hitting a pillowcase.

Now you're well rested. Wide awake.

Strapping on a watch, something any man would strap on, you cue up your music. A local hip-hop artist will top your list. One who lost his life to an overdose a few years ago. You'll hear his words as he rhymes under the name Oliver Hart, with the album's many references to the great river that divides Minneapolis and St. Paul.

As your breath bounces off the small fraction of a face showing through the ski mask, ice begins to cling to your frosty eyelids. You'll reach up with your hands and melt them away, simmering as you settle into your stride the sting that you chose not to leave this state behind to rest out west in the heart of Santa Monica sunshine. You'll hear the music through your earbuds like a message in a bottle, sending you love signs, reminding you it's not your time.

You'll try to believe it, but the ache in your lower abdomen is only complicated by the pain seething through your hip flexor area. You've noticed your right foot scraping your left ankle while running for some time. You've been having falls while running for months. You even fell during the marathon in October at mile 7, just to get back up with a gravel-filled kneecap and a blood-streaked shin, to run 19 more miles to the finish, spasms and all. You've been bringing the docs pictures of your injuries. You're getting injections in more places now as your baseline Botox dosage continues to increase. But you're still falling when you run. And the pain of trying to offset it, by overcompensating—step through the snowy paths, hop icy curbs, and fight the tears that seem to squeeze you but won't flow whenever you can't force your body to fly right and fight through.

The emotional load is taking its toll.

You'll turn back, thinking how tired you are of fighting an illness that threatens not to kill you like cancer but strip your life of meaning or pride.

You'll hear the river references in your ear and respond to the melodic cues. "It's not your time," you'll tell yourself. But your shoes take you to the bridge anyway. Almost as if the shoes you tied on are now running you. If you can't run, you aren't alive. It's been your motto since you got sober.

Why carry on and keep fighting when you've been losing, piece by piece, every meaningful thing in your life? You'll try to escape the questions, but you won't be able to. Your thoughts will just keep getting darker as you approach the halfway point on the bridge. You have no awareness of any plan. You haven't questioned where you're going.

Until now.

As you look down.

You'll see your life's snapshot frozen before your eyes, subliminal messages infiltrating your consciousness, as your pupils struggle to connect with the icy river, sixty-six feet below. You'll feel your stomach drop the full distance, your heart begging to seamlessly slide with it. You'll realize the railing to the bridge isn't where your arms expected it to be, as you are now perched on a small patch of snow that has raised your short height by a good six inches. You'll clench the railing with frozen fingertips once you find it, feet better positioned to jump than run. You'll be caught off guard by that transition. By your transition. By your cat's slow transition to the next world.

*By the fact that you're standing on a bridge at 4:45 a.m. on a frigid Febru-
ary morning, overlooking the mighty Mississippi, contemplating jumping.*

You'll think of your first book. You referenced Catcher in the Rye. *No
public suicides for this guy, right? You'll remember that your first book has
been a burden. Textbook or teaching tool, it's still vanity. A memoir. A
stain on the writing credentials you'll never attain. You'll remember that
all you've ever really wanted to be in life has been two things: a real boy and
a real writer. You wonder if you'll ever become either.*

*You'll think about your book, your cat, your mom. You'll even think
about your psychologist. You'd told her you were having these thoughts
again. You told her this bridge by your apartment had a pull on you.*

*Tears will try to flow, but they'll clot from the testosterone. Those that
do surface will refreeze to your cheeks should they get beyond your eyelids.
You'll reach up again with the same frozen fingers to chip away the icicles
caked to your long eyelashes. You'll take one step back and look back over
the ledge once more before turning your shoes pointedly in the direction of
your apartment.*

*In a few days, you'll hear the coffee pot steam at 3:47 a.m. The bridge
will still be here. And you'll tie on your shoes once again.*

OVER THE COURSE of weeks, the thoughts would come and go. I'd lace
up my women's running shoes, a cruel punishment at times that has required me to take a Sharpie to the colors, and find myself at the bridge.
Suicide—my own and the act thereof—seemed to be constantly on my
mind. My isolation persisted, and I avoided social media. Until I decided not to. A childhood friend messaged me on Facebook:

My dad died by suicide in March.

I just . . . wanted you to know.

She didn't need to say much more. My mind shifted. I thought back
to the emails her dad wrote me when my first book came out. I remember still how my growth and transformation in sobriety had affected
him. I thought of the fact that Mike was closer to me than my own
stepdad back in my basketball days. Of how supportive he had been as
a father figure and soccer coach. I looked at his Facebook page and saw
he had only one interest that he'd "liked": me.

18

Man at Work

With the eventual spring thaw came renewed hope. Hope that, perhaps, my running struggles could be resolved. I went in for my every-eleven-weeks Botox visit at the university, to be nailed like a two-by-four with needles from neck to lower leg, and updated Tanya, my care coordinator. With a warmth complemented by comprehensive clinical knowledge, she was the perfect point person for my complex neurological and orthopedic issues. We'd been working together for five years.

As usual, we went over how the cycle went. How much improvement of pain I had. How much relief from the muscle pulling I felt. I responded with similar reports of overall relief but yet another fall. I produced pictures, bloodied road rash and all.

I'd also mentioned to her that I felt torqued at the trunk and it even seemed I was turning while sitting to pee. The urgency and frequency I'd experienced in the few months postcoma were back, too, though they seemed connected to the Botox cycle. Dystonia does not impact smooth muscle such as the bladder, though, and Tanya seemed equally as surprised by the mention of my now very masculine self needing to sit to pee. I do. As Tanya had told me with complete honesty when I first started the transition process, "Please forgive us, Nate. We're old, and we're just not used to this yet." Seeing a body changing before them in a way unrelated to the condition they were treating had to complicate the clinical picture, since testosterone was having an enormous impact on my muscles.

But, fortunately, the muscle I was developing from testosterone was not all abnormal in tone. That is, it was not dystonic. It just seemed the dystonia itself was progressing, including in muscles that were, in fact, growing from testosterone. It also seemed more and more that the falls weren't originating from my foot or lower leg but rather from contractions in my side and lower abdomen.

She wheeled her stool closer to me and asked me to stand. I did, illustrating with a sweeping motion the wrapping around sensation of the pull that seemed to be twisting my trunk to the right and forward. She could see it and put her hands on my hips.

"Stand straight," she directed. Her once blond hair was starting to grey in a blended fashion, which for some reason furthered my trust in her. I tried to stand straight, find the position. But I couldn't do it. A physical therapist by background, she turned my pelvis to align me.

"Can you hold that position?" she asked, letting go.

As much as I tried to balance the tug of war pull on my abdominal, hip, back, neck, and shoulder muscles, I couldn't. My neck bent, my trunk torqued, I leaned, my abdomen curled, and my right hip turned—all inward, but in a way that would likely only be noticeable to the trained eye, or after being pointed out. I'd grown so accustomed to trying to fight the pull of the dystonia that giving into it, especially in front of providers, was unnatural.

For every other condition in my life, I needed to put up a front and show stability. Here I needed to let the condition take control of the same body I'd been fighting so hard to find control over.

"I feel like this is in my trunk," I said yet again. The previous round included shots in the lower leg, which seemed to help but hadn't fixed the falls or reduced the stress on my hip. "Here," I said, pointing to a visibly taut strand of abdominal muscle, made more pronounced by bending to my left. "This area is the pivot point." Much like twisting a rag with two hands, my body seemed to be torquing right in the middle, causing some muscles to pull one way while competing muscles pulled the opposite way.

That pull, and orthopedic issues, were carefully taken into consideration by Dr. Garramone during chest surgery. He'd placed my right arm in a different position. My left arm was placed in a normal position, though. Perhaps the insidious progression of the torque of my trunk had been causing the pull on that scar line on my left side. It was a consequence of chest surgery I never foresaw before going under the knife. In fact, it took almost a year for a portion of the left nipple graft to stay healed, and the left suture line was still struggling to stay closed entirely some eighteen months postsurgery. Something had to give in the force of the pull of my body at the end of each cycle, when my posture would return to its regularly scheduled abnormalities. Scar tissue and newer flesh would make the most sense as to where things would give way.

Tanya reached up and asked me to take off my shirt, a task far more comfortable for her by this point. With skillful grace, she palpated my lower right abdomen. Her usually warm expression turned to concern and then settled into sadness, corners of the eyes dropping as she moved along the muscle fibers with her fingertips. She continued on, touching muscles I felt were abnormally hardened, running like angled strands of rope from my ribs to my pelvis. She reached around my side as she continued, looking up at me.

"Oh, Nate," she said, shaking her head. "We need to treat this."

I TOOK THE pokes in the abdomen, where one wrong jab could mean a paralyzed diaphragm or a belly of Botox, and bent to my left as they injected rock hard strands of muscle all around my right side. Like a balloon, the muscles were so tight and taut they seemed to almost pop inside the sensory sounds of my own muscle fibers, resisting the tension brought on with the insertion of each needle.

The EMG machine, affixed to the needle and myself, measured the electrical current in my muscle. With each stick, it rumbled erratically before settling into the sound of a race car revving around a track. It's a sound I've come to learn is equated with dystonic, or abnormal, muscle tone activity. As a result, NASCAR has even less appeal to me than it already did.

THE ABNORMALITIES IN my muscle tone can be felt, much as I'd felt the abnormal nature of the lump on Ferrick just two months after selling the house. It was just another few weeks after passing on the Santa

Monica offer and making the short move across town to the haunted apartment that he took another decline. The stress of a third move in eighteen months could kill him. But I had to get out of that creepy apartment, away from its creepy landlord, and off the beckoning suicide bridge.

I was already struggling to manage my economic health due to advancing disability, and a move would be costly. I'd appealed for help from the state to be "certified" as disabled. It wasn't a move my pride wanted to make, but it was a necessary one. Some time before my psychotic frolic into despair, I got curious about the status of that application, which had been placed months earlier and had the potential to save me thousands on health care each year. It was still pending when I'd last checked into it. At one point during my mental health downfall, during which I managed to avoid hospitalization through the carefully honed art of acting "fine" and "normal," people from the state and then the county came to my creepy apartment building and did some assessments on me.

I don't remember much of those visits. But apparently my physical and mental health together were enough to qualify me as disabled under the same definitions used by the Social Security Administration. Being certified disabled by the State Medical Review Team in Minnesota opened new options for my health care. It would allow me to obtain a waiver to get additional help at home, and it would also allow me the luxury of just being able to pay a premium each month and have others handle the barrage of health-care-related tasks in my life.

One program, called Medical Assistance for Employed Persons with Disabilities, was a perfect fit. It encouraged people just like me to work despite disability. And unlike Social Security Disability, which only allows a very minimal and unlivable income each month, this program would have no income limit at all. The premium would simply be adjusted based on how much I was earning.

Along with its benefits, this new health care program also created new issues and caused others to resurface that I'd run into before. On the one hand, Mindy started taking state health care with the rollout of the Affordable Care Act, and I could see her again. But transgender services were not covered by Minnesota at the time. That meant the struggles I was having in even getting my testosterone and injection supplies could be amplified.

Like changing the Comcast bill name, getting supplies for my T had already proven itself a comedy—albeit a frustrating one. Once I ended up with 3-milliliter syringes to inject 0.13 milliliter, which would be like trying to measure a teaspoon using a quarter cup. That's a recipe for a bad cake and a serious medication dosing error. Another time I was told I could only get one-tenth of the hormone I usually got because I could only get a month's supply. I tried to do the math with the pharmacist, who surely knew calculations, but he wrestled to see how 0.26 milliliter x 4 would be greater than 1 milliliter, which is what I'd been given. Yet I was sent out the door that same day with a box of a hundred needles when a month's supply of those would have been a whopping total of eight.

Being on the state health care program for people with disabilities also opened new choices, and dilemmas, for housing. Most housing for persons with disabilities, I discovered, overlapped with senior housing options. As much as I love seniors, and as much of a hit as I was becoming with the eighty-five-year-old ladies, I wasn't sure I wanted to live in the same building with them, where I'd likely just end up an errand boy for my neighbors. Those options that weren't senior housing had either an outrageous wait list or were in areas conducive to relapsing on drugs. I chose to bypass that potential and returned to the building I'd lived in prior to the Santa Monica snafu.

I was tired of making decisions.

Eventually, though, program rules would require me to do just that. Billed as an incentive-to-work program, the MA-EPD option gave me the help I needed to excel in other areas of my life, including work. Yet it eventually requires you to file Social Security Disability. If the program is an incentive to work, why force people like me to declare they're too disabled to engage in any type of "gainful employment"? That "gainful employment" limit, or the income limit the Social Security Administration sets on monthly wages allowable while on SSDI, is ridiculously low. And just as being in subsidized housing would not be good for me, being on SSDI, unable to pursue work endeavors as I wanted, would not help my mental health.

I had to keep working as much as I could, as long as I could.

As I FEARED, Ferrick declined soon after the return across town closer to Cedar Lake, a spot where I'd come to feel at home during my transition. I watched him carefully in the days soon after we settled back into a building I knew as familiar but that he certainly didn't. Being as sensitive to death as I am, I wanted to give my best feline companion of twelve years a comfortable passing. I did not want him to suffer.

He still enjoyed watching the birds and squirrels, snuggling, and just doing cat stuff. He still had a routine and a quality of life—until it started to change. I took him to the vet, unsure if it was time. To the contrary, the vet noticed his nonverbals: His eye contact with me. His desire to leave her space and be in mine. As soon as she finished the exam and let up the stethoscope, he scurried to my side of the rectangular exam table and sat down, right in front of me, looking at her as if to say, "I belong over here with my human."

The vet gave a slight chuckle. "What I see here is a cat that wants to go home. He wants to stay in your sphere a little while longer yet."

My *sphere*. The phrasing stuck with me. His sphere—what composed his life—had gotten smaller and smaller, as had mine. But together we still stayed within the same sphere. Two weeks later, he helped make the decision for me. He gave me signs.

I knew it was time.

Rather than mourn, I chose to celebrate. As I'd learned to grow more comfortable working with human death, I thought often of what a blessing it is to be able to put down an animal to prevent or cease suffering. Through that, we can give them an everlasting gift of a peaceful and dignified death.

For some reason, we struggle to offer this for humans. Even when our loved ones are degenerating from diseases like dementia into states of mind and physical conditions that person might not consider to be livable, we keep them alive.

At Gables, in the months following my friend Mike's suicide, a resident who had been a brilliant engineer approached me with great intent several times, his face masked from the progression of his illness. He was short in stature, his hair grey on the sides as well as what little was left on top. The smile he'd once greeted me with eventually disappeared. Perhaps it was the rigidity of his muscles. Or perhaps it was because he knew what he wanted, despite his cognitive state. His statement each time was slow, monotone, but clear and consistent: "Just kill me."

How does one respond to such a statement from someone who has no hope of recovery? No chance of even maintaining the status quo? He seemed to know his brain was not functioning right, that his quality of life had been stripped away, just as his dignity was rapidly being shredded as well. He was losing continence, finding himself stuck in corners with his walker, and increasingly unable to enjoy intellectual pursuits that gave him great pleasure.

He used the same words each time. But I felt hit in the gut when he approached his final time. I told him the usual, about how things weren't easy and he was facing challenges, but we'd help make sure to honor his dignity and brighten his days. I also told him I'd been in places emotionally where I'd felt the same. Out of necessity, I asked about any plans or intent. Rather than shake his head and stand by my side, as he had in times past, he shuffled his walker to the right and turned away, saying nothing. No shake of the head.

He'd said fewer words over time and would say even fewer going forward, just as Ferrick ate less and less. Then, on August 12, Robin Williams died by suicide. The actor and comedian had struggled with mental health challenges and addiction, and had been aware that he was living with a form of dementia, most likely a rapid, progressive, devastating form called Lewy Body. It often causes significant mental health symptoms, namely hallucinations. Having gone psychotic myself, I knew how scary that was.

Psychosis was scarier than any drug trip, crash, high, or comedown, and I have no doubt Robin Williams felt that, too. I applauded—and still do—his courage to end it his way. On his terms. His actions are different than a preventable suicide of someone who does not want to die but is crying out for help. But where seeking help ends and wanting to die begins is a grey area. And where one crosses the line to having been through enough to justify suicide is even blurrier.

With animals, though, we humans decide when they've had enough. So I decided for Ferrick. As we awaited our appointment and mourned along with the world the loss of an entertainment industry icon, we spent one last night together and had a slumber party.

He sat on the bed as I told stories. I cued up some music and sang to him. Though he turned down every delicacy I offered him, I offered him what I was having: ice cream. He'd never had human food in his life until he got sick. At that stage, whether human or animal, why not let them enjoy something delicious even if it's not the healthiest option? Much as with my residents at Gables, I could only make him comfortable. But unlike my residents, I could help him find an end to his pain.

The next morning, I took him to the vet for the final time and said good-bye to my best friend.

The ensuing hunger and loss consumed my heart, swallowing it in an ache unmeasurable. It felt as if I were dying inside. It hurt nearly as bad as the loss of my ten-year relationship. Though it wouldn't occur to me until sometime later, I wasn't mourning only Ferrick when I put him down that day but also the final tie he represented to my life with Krissy.

JUST A FEW weeks after Williams's and Ferrick's deaths, my engineer friend at Gables also ended his pain. Though some may believe people with dementia lose the ability to carry out a suicide plan, I disagree. Much as with Robin Williams, I believe this was his wish. The collision of apparent suicides around me served to remind me that I, myself, was not actively suicidal.

I was on the upswing. I wasn't going to feel bad about feeling good when others around me were struggling, either. I was finally starting to find some reasons to stick around.

The addition of Botox treatment in my lower abs and right side proved successful. As I got into the summer long runs for yet another fall Twin Cities Marathon, the falls had stopped. I wasn't even scraping my ankle bone to a bloodied knob anymore. And since I was no longer compensating, the hip pain also resolved.

I went from struggling through a five-mile run in the frozen winter to being able to do eighteen-mile training runs again—without needing to stop for a dystonia break. The dramatic change not only opened me up to wanting to pick up more hours at work but also once again allowed me to enjoy my greatest pleasure in life: to simply run free.

Except for in the shoe department.

In that arena, I still had feet too small for men's shoes anywhere—in person or online. I settled for boys' boots. But for running shoes and other shoes, I had to go with women's. For years, the only colors to choose from were pink, purple, aqua, or some blend thereof. I finally wrote Asics a letter and told them that as a trans man, I still had a narrow heel and small feet. I needed a good fit to run marathons. But I asked them to please consider more gender-neutral color options.

Much the way the Twin Cities Marathon removed the F gender marker the year after I requested to run as Nate before my legal name change, running shoes started coming out more and more in gender-neutral colors. I surely had no part in why that all changed, but the small drop in the ocean of consumer voices was turning to a wave. People were starting to hear, and see, the power of the trans community.

I, in turn, was truly starting to look and feel like a man. People weren't seeing me as trans any longer. The only place people seemed to mistake my gender was on the phone, which I understand, since our voices often sound higher on the phone. The combination of the welcoming cultural atmosphere, improved physical functioning, and change in appearance was invigorating. My talks through NAMI were taking off as well. The more confident I felt in front of people, the more confident I felt inside. And I was finally starting to find the confidence to date again.

I'd fast discovered that being transgender is a divisive characteristic. My identity is a sexual fetish to some. An object of rape, rage, and murder for others. It can even be an obstacle in friendships. Though I'm attracted to women, I also tend to have women friends.

Just as I was unliked, unfriended, and the like right after coming out, the change in my appearance started to interfere with some of my friendships with women. Nobody questioned my motives or intent when I was a woman who was friends with women, regardless of any orientation or marital status. But as a man, that changed.

I may have still looked young for my age, but it was there. I could see a combination of both of my brothers forming in my own appearance. From the cheekbones to thick Adam's apple and facial hair, the shift had occurred. I was a man by all appearances. Proud of no longer feeling like a lost boy, I started posting more pictures online and was shocked by the number of compliments about my appearance. Most of them came from women.

Whether I physically look more attractive as a man than when I was a woman and playing the role of a woman, I do not know. I feel like a man. That's all that matters to me. Perhaps it's that confidence that gets confused with attractiveness.

But for the men married to or dating my female friends, my identity became a challenge. One friend directly told me, "My husband isn't comfortable with me talking to you anymore." Nothing had changed about our interactions, but how others were viewing me was changing what was expected of me. It was not expected that a single, straight man be friends with heterosexual women. In fact, it's more expected that I would *not* be.

Being transgender made me acutely aware that being friends with women would be different now, just as it would be with men. Any guy I'd become friends with would need to know up front I was trans. I could not live with that fear. Not in a friendship sense. And not in a romantic sense.

I was fast finding out that, in addition to the realm of friendship, there are things a lot of women want from a man that ruled me out as potential dating material from the get-go.

Namely, I lack a real penis. The clitoris grows a few inches on T. What flesh that develops looks and feels like any other penis, but it's not quite the same thing. It gets swollen and engorged, essentially erect, but has no ability to ejaculate. It's a sad reality that, for me, the only place I have a true cock is in my head, from dystonia.

It had always been more important to me to not have breasts than to have a penis. With my body and brain starting to come into alignment, what I lacked below the waist was becoming a much more pressing issue. Bottom surgery, as it is often called, could allow me to have use of a true penis to stand to pee and, I hoped, for sex. That seemed just as important as being able to stand to pee. But the saying I've heard in the medical community is that it's easier to dig a hole than build a pole. The penis is loaded with blood vessels. It also helps negotiate the urinary output system for men. Bottom surgery for trans men is usually many surgeries, with skin grafts taken from other body parts used to construct the penis.

I wasn't sure I wanted to go through with any of that just to have frequent urinary tract infections and a half-hard dick, but I had to ask if it was an option.

The intersection of my gender and disability put me at a stop sign once more. The Botox was helping me run once again, but it was not helping me sit straight. I was still crooked, even when peeing. And having to sit to pee was starting to challenge my mental outlook on life as a trans man, especially with public bathrooms, much the way running with a sports bra had years prior.

On my next visit to Dr. Thorp, I explained the peeing issues, as well as the uncomfortable sensations. She stayed silent, which always makes me feel I'm supposed to say more. Perhaps it's from years of therapists and professionals saying, *Say more about that!* So I said more. I told her I'd been dating again, even though it'd been a challenge to find someone who could see beyond my five-foot-two height, weird neurological condition, mental health challenges, and gender.

"I can't feel her, though," I said, leaning forward. Dr. Thorp looked at me with empathy, likely having heard this from other trans men time and again. "I want to feel myself inside her."

A strap-on harness, when made for trans men and when accompanied by a realistic dildo, is, for many, the best alternative. It can feel like an extension of the body. My brain and body knew where things were supposed to be.

The dystonia, Dr. Thorp noted, had progressed into the lower abdominal muscles that press right up against my bladder. "That could explain the urgency and frequency," she said, and the torque of the muscles would likely always be an issue. I'd probably always sit slightly crooked, in chairs and while peeing, too.

The peeing could be resolved, though. Through bottom surgery. I hoped the other pieces could, too. I pleaded my case and inquired about my suitability for surgery. She shifted her weight and tightened her lips. I already knew the answer.

"I don't think bottom surgery is going to be an option for you," she said. "The anesthesia and the heart rhythm is just one piece. Then there's the skin grafts, and with the dystonia, I just don't think it's wise."

Though the parts inside of me matter less than those on the outside, and a hysterectomy would seem unnecessary since I've put my body into menopause via T, occasionally I still do get menstrual cramps. And even more often, I've wondered how the collision of having female reproductive organs with male hormonal chemistry could impact my body's physiology.

It wouldn't have come as a surprise if it already had. My mental health was definitely affected. Since transition, some mental health traits that were more pronounced when I was a woman were settling down, while traits more common to males were emerging. I no longer seemed to need to be in an intense relationship or even be in one at all. Instead, I was having trouble committing to much more than sex. Yes, there was passion in my sex life. But it didn't translate into love anymore.

The disconnect from the intensity of emotion I'd become accustomed to as a woman was almost scary. Along with a reduction in emotional intensity in relationships, I was becoming more paranoid and reclusive. I retreated inward instead of sharing things with friends. And for as much as I wanted to, I could no longer cry as I used to, unable to tap into the well of tears that once cleansed me.

Unfortunately, the emotional impact of hormone therapy, complicated by bipolar and brain injury and a strong personality, was still compromising my anger management skills, albeit not as greatly. Dr. Thorp was pleased I'd been seeing Dr. Wiersgalla, the psychiatrist she referred me to.

Dr. Wiersgalla had confirmed Mindy's impression of bipolar I, mixed episodes, moderate to severe. We'd tried several meds, both anti-epileptics and mood stabilizers, and she worked closely with my neurologist to find meds that would not worsen my dystonia. Each med set off a sequence of side effects altogether too familiar, including pressing suicidal thoughts.

I couldn't stand it. I refused to keep taking them. I had to get off the pharmacological merry-go-round. Dr. Wiersgalla, to my surprise, agreed. "Fewer meds might actually be best for you," she noted. She continued to write a prescription for Adderall, though, as it had proved helpful for my ADHD for quite some time. Numerous rounds of neuropsych testing confirmed that diagnosis, as well as the brain injury components. Of my concerns, I'd told her my anger was the biggest. She'd encouraged me to bring it up with Dr. Thorp.

"They just approved a new pellet injection," Dr. Thorp explained. Called Testopel, the procedure would involve placing a small pellet into the gluteus muscle, the big butt muscle, which would dissolve over time and be repeated every three months. It would eliminate the need for weekly T injections at home. The guys at the Florida retreat who were from Europe and Canada had talked about how stupid it was that the United States didn't allow pellet injections.

I'd come in to see Dr. Thorp at just the right time. Or maybe the wrong time. I didn't get approval for a penis. But I got approved to have my butt cut open to have a pellet placed in the muscle that most helps me run.

The procedure itself, scheduled just a few days before the marathon, turned out to be far from an injection. Rear exposed but numbed, on my left side on an ob-gyn bed, I looked behind me expecting to see a needle. Instead I saw a pair of bloodied gloves, one of which was maneuvering a scalpel.

I didn't need to see any more to know this was more than just a little pellet. This was a marble. "Sorry this is taking me longer than usual," Dr. Thorp said, as if I'd know how long it usually took her. "I have to inject this into the fat under the skin, of which you have all of about 1 millimeter." Geesh. Even my good doctor was taking shots at my skinny frame.

She had a point, though. Being skinny and lean meant there was little fat to cushion the marble. The pellet was supposed to be pain free, not cause any side effects, and give a steadier dose of testosterone over time. Instead, it had the opposite effect.

"Butt hurt yet?" Brandi texted on the night of the procedure. It didn't yet. But it would once the anesthesia wore off. She'd warned me about doing this before the race, but Dr. Thorp assured me it would be fine. It wasn't. It challenged yet another marathon, as a marble swollen up to a ping-pong ball bounced off my butt muscle, right under my skin, with every step. Still, I trudged through as always and finished, deciding almost immediately afterwards to register for the Los Angeles Marathon just five months later. By then, I'd no longer have a pellet in my ass or be falling on my face.

In the end, the pellet resulted in raised lab levels that pushed my hormone levels all out of whack. It challenged my anger just as much as in my Hulk days, but unlike weekly injections, there was no come-down. With once-weekly shots, the levels rise, peaking about halfway through the week, and then drop. It's a roller coaster but one I'd found coping mechanisms to manage. I knew what days I was more inclined to be an asshole. But with the pellet, I was an asshole every day for weeks, and I had no sense of when that intensity was going to quell even slightly. That wasn't even to mention my baseline bipolar days of being an asshole. It also exacerbated my dystonia, which wanted me to sit right where the pellet was, but I instinctively fought against the dystonia to get away from the pain of sitting on the pellet.

After allowing me to vent about the failure of the pellet experiment, Dr. Thorp apologized. My complexities seemed to be putting me in her office with frequency. Many trans men never see an ob-gyn and, as a result, often run higher risks of cervical, breast, or other gynecological cancers. I certainly wasn't avoiding doctors. To the contrary, I couldn't get away from them. This pellet thing was a nightmare.

"I am *so* sorry," she said again, shaking her head. "I had no idea that was going to happen." I don't know if she meant the hormone levels or the pellet fucking with my dystonia, but either way, we both agreed: never again.

"Why don't we go to twice-weekly shots?" she suggested. This way, I'd be taking the same dose, just in a more spread-out fashion. One more needle every week. One more needle in my life.

I hesitated but agreed. It turned out to be a saving grace for my anger and emotional stability. After two years of trial and error and ups and downs, my hormones were finally getting settled. My mental health was figured out. My dystonia was under control. Even my heart rhythm was getting back to normal readings. With a new feline friend, Miles, I was making new memories. Starting anew.

Life was good.

Gables also seemed to be seeing my potential. I'd been working hard, hoping for the chance to move up the ladder, and was accepted to a Leadership Development program. It would take me to both Detroit and Chicago. My sister had lived outside of Detroit for years, and as our mom's health started to decline once more and her fairytale retirement in Asheville, North Carolina, dwindled, she moved with her husband to Michigan.

At the time the Leadership Group opportunity came around, I hadn't seen my mom in almost two years. It had just been too hard to get to North Carolina—physically, financially, and emotionally. So, too, it was becoming tough for her to even get to her kitchen, let alone fly to Minneapolis.

I approached the administration, which now included Gretchen. To my surprise, in her shift to an HR role, she hadn't been shipped off to Kansas or some remote island to undergo complete personality reprofiling. For once I could trust someone in a role that usually seemed to be out to get me. Gretchen's boss approved my request to stay a few extra days to visit family. Once in Michigan, the torture of eight-hour days in conference room chairs, with their shiny, happy little metal frames and no arms, fast grew exhausting. It's hard enough to fight the torque of my condition and the urge to slouch, and prevent any grimace when forced to sit for long, but to do so while still hiding pain and looking normal is almost impossible. I resisted the urge to ask for a nap mat and curl up on the floor. This wasn't kindergarten. This was my career.

Gables had consistently seen my dystonia as an asset, not a liability. As Gretchen had told me once, my condition gave me an insight and empathy that others didn't have. These weren't residents, though. These were some of the highest-ranking officials in the company. I had no interest in joining the other participants for drinks at the bar after all that sitting, either, and once more came up looking a bit like the loner. I didn't care. I did my thing. I made an impression, or at least I thought

I did, and left the conference with confidence. In pain, but with confidence. A step into management was the next logical goal.

MY SISTER PICKED me up to make the forty-five-minute drive back to her house, where we waited for our mom. It could be awhile. She wasn't moving very fast anymore. The wound on her leg that had developed after surgery, coupled with significant degeneration in her back and hips, made walking a near impossibility. Still, she fought for every ounce of her independence.

My sister and I talked superficially as my niece and nephew circled around the center island, snacking on crackers, asking Uncle Nate rapid fire questions. They were eight and ten at the time, and it seemed my gender was no big deal to them. My niece could remember when I was Jen. She seemed to have no issue with me being Nate, instead thinking people who didn't get it were "lame." My nephew just knew me as Nate. He didn't seem to care that I was once a woman. I could've been born a dinosaur, and he would've thought that'd been equally as cool.

They each clung to one side of me when the front door creaked opened, the fall breeze rushing in with it. I could hear my mom, her grunts of pain and the clank of her cane against the banister as she clawed for each step. She dragged her way up half a flight of stairs to the kitchen, letting out a sigh as she conquered her personal Kilimanjaro at the top of the staircase.

Short of breath, she stood still and stared at me. I stared back. And smiled. Disbelief seemed to jump off of her, diving into a fast-rising river of emotion. She quickly choked up and shook her head as if she'd just been given a gift she didn't expect.

I'd had to give her time. We didn't see one another. She chose not to look at many pictures. She hadn't seen me. She only heard the vocal changes on the phone, infrequently.

Feeling her emotion, I removed my niece and nephew from their spots at my side and went around the island, headed in her direction with swift steps and open arms. She squeezed me in a tight hug, a comfort only a mom can provide—one I'd long forgotten, and missed.

The tears streamed down her cheeks as she let go of the embrace and reached up to dab a tear from her eye with the Kleenex she always seems to have an extra of.

"You look just like your dad," she said, voice quivering. "You've turned into such a handsome man." She took a moment to just examine me, beaming ear to ear.

A parent. Proud of her son.

It took her a full two years, but her words sealed it. She'd found acceptance. I'd known there was nothing I could do to speed the process along, as much as I'd ached for it. She'd accepted me throughout addiction and mental health challenges, supported me with hockey, and never turned her back on me no matter how difficult I was to manage. But this time, as I was finding my own identity, I had had to give her space, going much longer than I usually would between communications, to let her grieve the child she wished to reel back in. It took time, work, and patience on my part to understand her position. It took the same for her. But she also needed to see the happiness that beamed from my face, the naturalness in my own gait, and my general comfort in my clothes and skin. The upwards swing of my career didn't hurt, as vocational success is yet another marker of a man in our society, and especially in my family. But more than anything, she needed to see the physical changes. She needed to be able to look at me and see what others would visibly decipher as a man in order to be comfortable. That same discomfort with uncertainty engulfed the kids I'd worked with, just as it did the two boys at the Y.

Somewhere while I was cruising along through this journey of transition, though, I turned a corner. The question of "Is that a man or a woman?" answered itself. If I were to identify as genderqueer, choose to remain androgynous, or go by pronouns such as "they" or "them," I don't think it would be nearly as easy for my mom to accept my decision to transition. She would see the ambiguity as indecision, which is largely a reflection of her generation's thinking. But she also thinks in very black-and-white terms, much the way we, as a society, separate the boy and the girl. We want certainty. Finally, she had that certainty she so needed.

Over those few days, she watched the way I carried myself, how I smiled, talked, moved. "This is right for you," she said when we had our departing hug. "It should have been this way all along."

19

Invisible Man

Sometimes I can still sense where they were, their exact location and placement. If I bring my hands up to touch my chest, my fingers and palms still instinctively know where they sat. They travel along the same space they once occupied. Sometimes when I roll over in bed, I still maneuver so as not to pinch them, even though they are gone, long since severed from the same skin that binds the very flesh that once covered them.

I often wonder, where are they now? Are they on a woman's body? Sewn and woven into the skin of another? Someone who needs and wants them far more than I ever did? Or could they be in a medical warehouse, Walmart-style, where aisles of breasts are labeled A to DD? Do scientists push squeaky grocery carts, pondering which jar to pick, while overhead pages announce the sale prices on penises?

Or are they being kept in the bowels of an institution in a dusty lab where white-haired people wear white coats? Are they being used for research? Are they being used to help teach humans how to analyze skin, flesh, cells? Perhaps a first-year med student threw one down on a frigid, sterile cutting board and sliced off a section to examine it, his eyelashes twitching against the nameless lens of a microscope as he stared at my tits.

Up close. Yet otherworldly. The last human to look at, let alone touch, my breasts. Boobs. Whatever you call them, they're now jarred. Preserved with chemicals, like pickles on a sticky counter at a corner dive bar.

My naked upper body now reflects my true gender. What I don't have below the waist doesn't make me any less of a man, either. But the fact that my female origins became invisible to the untrained eye, just like my dystonia and my bipolar, doesn't mean that history doesn't exist. The realities of living with mental health challenges, unusual physical limitations, and being transgender hit me daily.

Like the tornado that hit my house as a youth, cycles of destruction and rebuilding have shaped my life. Just when I think I have it figured out, something whisks the rug out from under me, and I fall flat on my face. I've literally had to pick myself up after each fall. But for once in my life, I finally felt I was starting to stand on stable ground.

I've encountered hate and will continue to encounter it. I'll still struggle with suicidal thoughts and anger. I'll wrestle at times with my body image, and my neurological illness will remain progressive. I, like everyone, will live the rest of my days in complete uncertainty regarding my future. Yet, as hard as it is sometimes, I continue to stay in the race.

It means the world to me that I've helped inspire others to change their own lives or shift their perspectives. But it would mean much more to know that I don't always have to be Superman. I can just be Clark Kent—if Clark Kent were a dystonic trans guy with brain injury and bipolar.

All any of us have is who we are. I was starting to find peace enough within my mind and body to be able to enjoy at least some of the journey and not fixate so steadily on the final destination.

WORKING WITH DEMENTIA gave me that outlet. To be a part of death and dying in a way that gave back to others and also honored their individuality, just as I'd hope others would honor mine, was worth more than any paycheck. But Gables still didn't seem to have any interest in moving me up the ladder. I at least wanted to try my hand at a job with significant leadership responsibility, and it seemed that's what they were grooming me for. What was the holdup?

When tensions grew thick after a change in corporate leadership, I started looking for work elsewhere. I found a director-level position running a dementia unit at a skilled nursing facility, which fit my skill set well. I threw my hat in the metaphorical ring and got the job.

From the first day, I knew there was a stark socioeconomic difference between the residents in the for-profit skilled nursing environment, governed by Medicare/Medicaid services, and those in the for-profit private-pay world. These people were not rich. In any way. Many had been left by "loved ones" at hospitals, locked away in rooms or abandoned houses, exploited in every way. Even more striking was the markedly increased numbers of persons whose dementia was acquired by way of substance abuse, brain injury, or both. Most had an overlapping mental health diagnosis that had been established long before dementia set in. The life stories of the individuals I'd now be working with proved scarily similar to my own.

An early onset of depression. Sprinkle on a brain injury, perhaps by way of a suicide attempt. Mix in some drugs and alcohol. Suddenly you have a perfect storm. Just as my brain went haywire and developed dystonia, I was now seeing the aftereffects of a life of combined genetic predispositions and life choices that led to permanent consequences in the form of degenerative disease. This was the full circle.

I'd started out working with adolescents with mental health and substance abuse problems, then moved to an LGBT adult chemical dependency and mental health facility, and now to the end result: the nursing home. The place where we, in America, toss aside those we no longer wish to see and who are perceived as no longer bringing obvious value to our economy or society. We hide them away, tuck them on top floors, and keep them out of sight because they're out of their minds.

The path seemed all too clear. If you don't get your shit together as an adolescent or young adult, you'll end up in revolving treatments as a middle-aged adult, with economic challenges and strained relationships to boot. And if you don't get your life together then? You end up losing it all. The people at AA weren't kidding when they said that alcoholism would lead to jail, institutions, or death. More and more, the dementia unit was looking like a last-resort landing spot for homeless alcoholics and other medically complex cases that induced progressive cognitive loss.

Though I was still certified disabled, I wanted to *not* be perceived as having no obvious value or purpose. I wanted to be viewed, by others, as being a productive member of society. I also wanted to keep a roof over my head. Move up the corporate ladder. Use my intellect and experience to obtain a role that would make not only me proud but my mom as well.

It tugged at my soul as I grew to know the life stories of the new residents under my care, seeing the environment they were living in and knowing so many of them had absolutely nothing. Many relied on me to provide them with clothes. It reminded me how much I still had to give. How grateful I was to have made the decisions I did when I was younger to turn my life around with respect to chemical dependency and, later, my gender identity and mental health.

At some point, I donated my former women's wardrobe to some of the petite women on the unit. I also donated some of my old running shoes. It seemed a simple way to pay it forward and make sure that the clothes I no longer needed or wanted but couldn't seem to part with went to good use. The women I donated them to didn't need to know, nor would they likely process correctly, the fact that those had been my clothes when I lived as a woman.

Some things were better left unsaid.

With dementia, I didn't have to say anything about my gender, and nobody was going to figure it out. I looked, acted, and dressed like a man. That was all they needed to draw their conclusions about my gender, and increasingly the ladies were pinching my cheeks and rubbing my shoulder, letting me know what a sweet and "good lookin' guy" I was. Only my height and my shoe size caught the attention of one of my residents as being a bit off. Such discussion often brings on the question of age. Though people with dementia do ask how old I am and seem to be in disbelief when I tell them, cognitively intact persons also ask that question and seem equally jolted by my response. How could someone in their mid-thirties look twenty-one?

Transition seemed to have a youth-enhancing effect on my appearance. The slender jaw line became more squared—chiseled, soft, yet masculine. A blend that seemed to be getting more attention from onlookers and online commenters. But for all the superficial aspects people see, they don't see that, not only do I work my ass off, but the constant muscle contraction from dystonia actually raises my metabolism. A tough side effect to have, many might think, but I would trade it in to relieve the discomfort of my condition any day.

Over time, the power of the dystonic contractions have made me quite lean. The muscle is distributed differently from the testosterone as well, with even my forearms and wrists wider than they used to be. At times, it can be a challenge to maintain my weight, especially given my history of weight fluctuations when I was living as a woman and the unhealthy calorie-restricting coping mechanisms I'd developed as a teenage girl. It was sometimes a struggle to honor my need to eat more to fuel my adult male runner's body, but unlike in my youth, I wasn't trying to lose weight. I really was trying to maintain it.

Mindy questioned me about it more than once. "How has your eating been?" she'd ask. I insisted I was trying to graze more. Carry snacks like almonds with me. Eat before bed. I was eating full meals and ice cream. But as I adjusted to my new role as director, constantly on my feet and on the go in between meetings and calls, the weight continued to drip off.

I couldn't see it. But the doctors could.

I was, as I had been in 2012, in tunnel-vision mode. My career seemed to be taking off. I had to honor that and put in the work. But between work and graduate school, my body was starting to feel the effects of the stress. And also the political climate change.

Just as my weight and how society perceived it and my body had now changed, so too began the wave of political pushback against the trans community in early 2016. Society. Perceptions. It's all dependent. Often changing. When I was still living as a woman, for instance, being skinny was considered an attractive feature. For a man, society has deemed it to be decidedly unattractive. Even Heather commented, on a visit to LA to run a marathon on Valentine's Day, that I was getting almost too thin—for a man.

The norms were different now.

If I were to have said, "That's a cute blouse," to a female colleague when I was a woman, lesbian or not, it would most likely not have been looked at as anything but a compliment. If I, as a man, compliment that same colleague with the same statement, my statement could easily be misconstrued as an advance.

I had to learn how to act as a man. There was no guidebook on Amazon or self-help site that was going to teach me. No lessons were needed on the actual *art* of being a man. It was a role I'd been dying to play.

Instead, it was the social norms. The new rules of behavior. The subtleties of language and mannerisms that govern our every action that I started to call into question. How the hell was I supposed to act? Suppose I approach a doorway at approximately the same time as a woman. Should I step ahead more quickly so to open the door for her? Or would that make me look like a desperate little dude trying to make an impression?

The hesitation of such menial yet crucial moments seemed to be stopping me in my tracks, though I was doing quite well on the running front. I returned to LA, sans pellet in the ass or spasms in my abs, finishing my ninth marathon with a personal best. My talks were taking off, and I'd even been able to fly my mom to Minneapolis to see me receive an award from NAMI for the speaking I'd been doing.

Everything seemed to be heading in the right direction, and I was accomplishing more than I could have imagined.

Soon after the race, though, I started to feel unwell. A sinus infection led to a chest cold that I just couldn't quite kick. The foggy brain and hangover from the trial and error of various sinus and allergy medications continued to thicken. But my thoughts were still clear on one thing: the messages I was receiving from the trolls that lurk on the internet and try to destroy your worth, your sense of belonging, and silence your voice were starting to increase in number.

The vast universe of the internet seemed to be turning into a hateful place. I withdrew from some social media accounts, as strangers, both via email and elsewhere, started taking shots at me. I wasn't sure where or whom to turn to for support. Though my career and reputation within the LGBT community seemed to be on the right track, I didn't think it was the right time to bring up any concerns about hate or discrimination, even to other LGBT folks, when the Pulse nightclub shooting in Orlando began to challenge our very notion of inclusion and visibility.

The very struggles of living with a complex, layered identity in a tumultuous sociological climate became the story. Despite gender identity (and disability) being in the center of a political spotlight and being on the receiving end of the backlash, I, and many others in the trans community, started to live behind a veil of silence once again. What voice could we have if we were merely going to be attacked for daring to be seen or heard?

With time I'd both learn and remember that in order to ever arrive at acceptance, we have to first be prepared for the pushback.

20

Premonitions

I drew open the same black shower curtain I'd had since my gender wres-
tles came to the surface some five-plus years earlier, far more at peace
with a flat chest, broad shoulders, and chest hair. No postshower boob
shake necessary now, some four years post–top surgery. As I tied a towel around my waist, looking past the reconstructed chest I continued to
pay off loans for, my hand brushed my inner thigh. There I felt a cord.

My fingers traced the taut stretch of wire, running like a guitar
string just beneath my skin, speed bumps dotting the course. It grew
firmer just a few inches above my knee. Bump after bump the guitar
string stayed taut as I drew my fingertips back up closer to my groin.
There, it disappeared from touch, no longer feeling pluckable. A gut
instinct stirred not a signal of pain but instead a subtle brew of discomfort mixed with alarm. It seemed to be sending a message: press here
and something very bad could happen.

I raised my leg to the bathroom counter to get a closer look, towel dropping to the floor in a heavy heap in the process. The pink
patch outlying the vein felt warm to the touch, full, almost swollen.
The purplish-blue vein was raised, palpably protruding with bumps
lining its visible course. Unsure what to make of it, I pulled out my
phone and took a picture, just in case, and lowered my leg back to
the floor.

Before I could even finish shaving my face, a now daily chore that
had turned out to be quite difficult because my neurological disorder
pulls my head to the right, an itch crawled through the skin of my left
leg where the vein was now commanding attention.

Over the next few days, I waffled. Working full-time in my role as a director of a dementia unit, I found it difficult to just up and leave for appointments. I couldn't even seem to find time to schedule them. After working a weekend, I took some free time during the business day to call Dr. Thorp, who manages my gender services, including hormone therapy.

By the time I mustered the courage to call, weird things had started to happen. A cord quite similar to the one running up my leg had popped up along my abdomen. When distended fully, it traveled up through my chest wall, my mastectomy scar, and right up into my armpit. There, just like with my upper leg, it disappeared. What was weirder was that when a cord was palpable below the waist, one wasn't above the waist. When it was above the waist, it wasn't palpable below. To top it off, I was still fighting off nonresolving X-ray–diagnosed pneumonia, worsened after a three-hour flight that left me coughing up blood again.

I knew I needed to see a doctor, but I hesitated. At the worst, I feared lung cancer. But I also wondered if I could have a blood clot that was getting into my lungs, a pulmonary embolism. Those either resolve and dissolve on their own, or they kill you. Not much in between. But more than that fear was the fear of having to explain all of this. Providers, and the staff who work for them, can be very dismissive of people like me: transgender people with complex medical issues and complex backgrounds whose identities don't fit neatly into tidy little boxes and whose diagnoses aren't well understood.

But Dr. Thorp and her staff had, to that point, been quite helpful with my array of complex issues. A few days later, sitting lakeside in the summertime, squinting through the sun piercing beneath my sunglasses, I found red streaks tracking along the outskirts of the raised blue highway running the course of my inner thigh. Another cord stretched up my chest wall through my left mastectomy line. Something told me this wasn't good. It wasn't resolving, and neither was my pneumonia. I picked up the phone, navigated through the maze that is the electronic voice prompt system, and eventually arrived at a human being for nurse advice. The woman on the other end of the line sounded impatient, her speech hurried as she greeted me.

I tried to speak more rapidly, which isn't necessarily a positive, since I tend to talk fast anyway. Despite the anxiety amplifying, I spit it all out. The vein, the pneumonia, the stuff I'd literally been spitting out. She interrupted more than once, in the end concluding, "I'm afraid this isn't Dr. Thorp's territory." Citing the vein issue, she encouraged me to seek out a vascular specialist.

I disagreed. "This could be a side effect of the testosterone, which she prescribes," I said. "Plus, this vein goes right up from my leg, to my abdomen, then through my mastectomy line. That's br—"

She interrupted again. "Did she do your gender reassignment surgery?"

"No." I got up to my feet in disbelief, trying to collect my thoughts, staring out at the open waters of Cedar Lake. "But she handles the health of my breast tissue." I was clear: it didn't matter if my mastectomy was because I'd had breast cancer, was trans, or any other reason, it was still my breast area. As a trans man post–double mastectomy, I still needed to get breast exams. And Dr. Thorp did those breast exams, as well as my pap smears. She would likely want to know if something was going on that could be related to the health of my breast tissue or complications from the medication she was prescribing.

The nurse wasn't having it. I was getting heated. I hung up the phone before the conversation was over, following up with an online message to my doctor to please recommend a primary care doctor who had nurses knowledgeable about transgender and neurological issues.

She replied and ordered an urgent ultrasound of my leg, which revealed a superficial blood clot in my left leg.

REALITY. EXPRESSION. WE express our reality by way of our gender expression or posture, our word choice and nonverbals. The very activities we engage in on a daily basis. But do we really express that reality? Is how we see ourselves more true or accurate than how others see us? To examine a sculpture without looking at all angles would obscure our ability to see things from all sides.

The nurse saw, in that portrait of a moment, a different reality from that which I was living. She saw signs and symptoms not typically associated with a call to the ob-gyn. She was understandably confused. Yet she also seemed to have little insight into the complexities of my issue and seemed unreceptive to hearing about them. Indeed, I didn't even know that just two years earlier, in 2014, a large-scale study done by the National Institute of Health showed an increased risk of blood clots, heart attack, and stroke with the use of testosterone.

We already knew that hormone therapy for women, including contraceptives, can increase the risk of clots and cardiovascular issues. It would seem logical that testosterone would do the same. The Mayo Clinic would go on to do a second, similar study, with similar results. It found testosterone increased the risk of heart attack and stroke but not blood clots—though curiously enough, blood clots can be the cause of heart attacks and strokes. I've often wondered, if I ever were having a heart attack or stroke, if my symptoms would present more like a man's or a woman's. Perhaps dystonia would make even that too complex to tell.

I didn't know about the studies when an inflamed pink cord popped up on my upper left leg. Or when, at the same time, I started coughing up blood, both bright red serum and deep crimson clumps.

This couldn't be my reality. It was just how the doctors were seeing it.

FIVE MONTHS LATER I received an email from my mom. She wrote that she needed to tell me she loved me. That she was proud of me for becoming the man I'd become. That she was going into major surgery to have hardware removed from her lower leg, which had left an unresolved open wound and bone infection called osteomyelitis. I had no idea the surgery had even been scheduled, but I knew that once she went in for it, there was a risk they would have to amputate her lower right leg.

She mentioned none of that but said that in her pre-op testing, they'd found an infarction on the EKG. She'd had a heart attack. It seemed to awaken her sense of mortality, a sense far too familiar to me after five years of working with aging and dying people and five years after my own death and revival.

Her words left an ache in my own heart. Rarely, if ever, have I seen such emotional content in written form coming from my mom. I had to sit with it for a few days to process it. I started a response then deleted it. I questioned how to respond, then rethought it again. Finally, I replied. Short, simple, sweet. For four more days I got no response. My anxiety swirled, mounting by the hour, confounded by the premonitions of death that sometimes keep me awake at night when one of the residents with dementia I've cared for is trying to communicate with me.

I get the feelings often. The sense that someone is trying to reach me. My anxiety quells to stillness, I feel a sense of relief or release, and I find myself shifting into thoughts of death.

Dust to dust, with a spirit drifting gently to wherever those we lose go to watch over us. These spirits, my guardian angels, call to me. They ask me to pay attention. To notice the lone honey bee on the sunflower that's opening to face the sun on a dewy spring morning. To take in the lilac scent wafting in the gentle breeze of an otherwise ordinary Minnesota day in May.

I COULDN'T SEPARATE out the messages I was getting. Was it a resident or my mom trying to communicate with me? Why did whoever was trying to reach me keep telling me something was wrong? If something was wrong with my mom, wouldn't my sister or brother contact me? They hadn't. Yet she hadn't replied to my last message. If something was wrong with one of my current residents, I'd know. Perhaps it was a former resident I'd worked with or a current resident in the hospital. None of those answers seemed to settle with me.

I emailed my mom once again and told her I was worried. I asked her to respond if she was able. She did not. I tried her cell phone but kept getting a "user busy" signal. The message from my brain was becoming more pointed: this is about your mom, the woman who brought you into this world and who is the reason you are still alive and breathing. This is not about work.

I couldn't ignore my gut any longer. If I did, I'd have to live with the potential regret for the rest of my life. But I'd ended the holidays with the intention of distancing myself from my family, particularly my siblings. They were the last people I wanted to reach out to with some weird gut instinct about our mom that they'd probably just write off as being a sign of mental illness anyway.

I had nowhere to channel my energy but everywhere and no place, all at once. Days became nights. Hours melted from the clock as I baked in my thoughts. I couldn't manage to write simple emails, read them, or stay on track in work meetings. I was walking to wrong buildings and missing turns while driving. I flat-out could not focus as the fear worsened. I knew I needed to find her and that my siblings weren't going to find me. And I certainly couldn't give 100 percent of myself to helping other seniors with needs, knowing in my heart that my mom needed my help.

She didn't leave the name of the hospital that was treating her. Didn't leave a number to reach her. Though I'd worked to get her into the University of Michigan, believing that my battles with dystonia may have served the purpose of affording me the knowledge needed to get her to the right doctors, I understood her primary doctor there had recently left. She'd also had procedures done in regional and county medical centers closer to her home outside of Flint. She could be anywhere.

I started dialing numbers. To clinics, main operators, directories, admissions coordinators. One call led to the next, then routed back to where I started. It seemed I was getting somewhere, though, eliminating possibilities. Eventually I got somewhere in the University of Michigan system. Another email to my mom sat without a response. But my brain demanded one—just as I got a direct number to her room.

BACK IN MINNESOTA, where a different U of M had tended to my own health issues, a trip to the hematologist had ruled out HIV, the emphasis on which seemed rooted in a stereotype about my drug addiction history and membership in the LGBT community.

What should be more important were my risk factors at that point, not those I had when I was younger. We are more than a medical record. We are unique, and there's a big difference between having cultural competence and practicing cultural humility.

Sometimes, though, we humans show universal signs that medicine has recognized. One such sign, the hematologist noted, is called the Trousseau sign of malignancy. It basically states that for over 150 years, we've known that recurrent, migratory blood clots can be a sign of cancer. The definition of the term has broadened, taken multiple meanings, strayed from its original intent. The sign, however, remains an important marker.

Upon receiving my negative HIV test result, I got a call from the hematologist herself. Though the words she used blur like the memory of the outside world events or even the weather of the day, one word stuck out: *cancer.*

THEY POPPED UP and down. From the upper leg on the left to the lower left abdomen, right up my abs and chest through the scar from chest surgery. On occasion, one popped up as a cord in my lower right leg. It migrated. It moved. It came. It went. By the day, by the hour. Usually I get right on medical tests, but with all the complexities of my situation, I hesitated.

These sorts of clots are most often associated with pancreatic cancer and lymphoma, the hematologist had noted. Indeed, pancreatic cancer is quite lethal. Testosterone is tough for the pancreas to process as well. Not only does my hormone therapy put me at more risk of clots in general, but it appears to cause chaos in the pancreatic region, which estrogen is then there to offset. I do not have any estrogen left to help protect the pancreas from fighting with the testosterone. At some point, something could go awry. A bar fight could break out. Perhaps it already had.

I avoided scheduling my next appointment, not exactly eluding phone calls but rather not following up on what was being recommended. It sounded like the odds of cancer were low, but the signs were there.

I LEFT WORK accompanied by my frantic gut instinct about my mom, too frazzled to check my email one more time before heading to St. Paul for class but with the number plugged into my phone, I picked it up and dialed. The thumping of my heart felt audible through my ear, pressed to the phone. She answered. "Hi mom," I said. I had to hide my concern. "How did the procedure go?"

Having no idea of my frame of mind, she explained that they'd found the infection in her bone, which was being caused by the hardware, and removed it successfully with no complications. She had avoided amputation on a leg with acute osteomyelitis, which had been brewing for a few years. That itself was remarkable.

"It was the other stuff that really threw me," she added. I asked if she meant the heart attack. She said no. In her tone I could sense a bit of uncertainty. "Did you get my email?"

I explained that I hadn't checked it in all of two or three hours. She'd emailed me during that time.

"Where are you?" she asked.

"Sitting in my car in rush hour on the way to class. What other stuff, mom?" Time seemed to stand still. As did the traffic.

"The cancer."

That word again.

"I'm sorry. Wait. What? What are you . . . What kind of cancer?" The second of silence before her answer seemed to stretch on for hours.

"Lung."

THE STILL COOL breeze of late winter clipped me at a greater depth when I arrived at school, numb, going through the motions. My tests, some four months earlier, had come back clean. No parasites or infections or weird things in my blood. No signs of cancer on any scans or smears. Just a few nodules in the lungs. Doctors assured me they were completely benign. Normal. "Likely just scar tissue from when you were using drugs or had your respiratory arrest." But due to my risk factors, I was told to schedule follow-ups with a pulmonologist.

In the time from my initial scans in October 2016 to my revisit in February 2017, my lungs had cleared from chronic infections. No more pneumonia or coughing up blood. Pulmonary function tests came back normal. But the aspirin, which had been upped to 325 milligrams from the baby dose of 81 milligrams, seemed to no longer be doing the trick. The weird clots were back. But this time one was pink and inflamed under my left arm, along the vein—and the mastectomy line.

I knew it wasn't the pulmonologist's territory, but it was these very clots that led me to the cancer workup in the first place, which ultimately led me to the pulmonology revisit. I showed him pictures and described it for him.

"I'm just a pulmonologist," he noted. *Just* a pulmonologist, I thought. Specialists tend to back away from anything outside of their area. "But I highly recommend you get back in to see hematology right away."

I hesitated. He insisted.

The next day, over a thousand miles away, different university doctors found a lump on my mom's lung they were "pretty sure" was cancer.

They were right.

Surgery, infection, medication, age. All factors that can contribute to abrupt changes in consciousness. I saw the subtle delirium when I visited her in the subacute rehab I specifically chose due to my own knowledge of how hideous things can be in the nursing home world. During my visit, she asked me what I'd be doing for supper while I was eating it. She was unable to stay awake to finish a sentence or to swallow a bite of food. She stopped eating altogether.

It's in moments like those that reality hits hard. For the person in the portrait and those who happen to also fall into the frame.

Her view is altered by her other health factors, like the fact that she quit smoking sixteen years ago and thought she was beyond any risks. My view of the picture is fundamentally altered by years of working in the field she now falls in, both in the skilled nursing area and in the social factors of insurance, in-home health care, and overall complexities of medical scenarios.

But it's also skewed by my own eerie ease with death and often distressing premonitions. Even my psychiatrist and psychologist have suggested I have psychic abilities. That is, I literally take on the feelings or emotions of others I'm connecting with. Perhaps I was feeling my mom's cancer, showing the signs via pneumonia and blood clots in a way not even she was. Perhaps I ended up in a university pulmonologist's office, with the words "surgery" and "oncology" and "lungs" and "cells" surrounding me, because just one day before, unbeknownst to me, different university doctors were looking at those same things on my mom. Perhaps I carried her warning signs.

Or perhaps she got lucky.

She was fortunate to have been in the hospital when she developed a cough that led to the scans that found the cancer right away. It was so early on that it was classified as Stage 1A. She had absolutely no symptoms.

It was a far different picture from the one I was looking at with the post-pulmonology follow-up, with red flags of cancer but no sign of it on any tests. I circled back to Dr. Thorp to let her know what the pulmonologist said and ask if she agreed. I suggested perhaps I should try a different compound for the testosterone. Maybe my veins were just sensitive to so many injections. She thought we could try it but agreed I should return to oncology. I tried my other doctors. Someone had to be able to tell me this wasn't a sign of cancer. But nobody could. Grasping at straws, I tried my psychiatrist. Maybe this was just in my head? She disagreed. As did my psychologist.

Five doctors. Same message. *Get thee to an oncologist!*

THE MESSAGE SANK in, just as news of my mom's lung cancer hit. I looked up the oncologist Dr. Thorp had recommended and discovered her to be a breast cancer specialist.

Breast cancer.

We weren't just looking for possible cancer now. I'd heard pancreatic, lymphoma, and lung, but not breast. This would change everything. We'd now be looking for cancer in the very tissue I had nearly lost my life because of, and which I'd just finished paying loans off to have removed. Finally, after decades of not belonging in the body I was born into, I was starting to feel like my body, my shell, was my own again. Now that same body seemed to be turning on me once more.

A cruel irony, especially given that treatment for breast cancer is often a mastectomy. Testosterone would also be contraindicated. Though the tests again came back cancer-free, the uncertainty remains unsettling. There is no question in my mind. If I, as a transgender man, ever develop breast cancer, and the only way for me to treat it would be to stop male hormones, which would amplify the femininity I nearly lost my life to rid myself of, I would refuse treatment.

Period.

Breast cancer is often considered a more curable form of cancer than lung cancer, where the word "cure" seems even more out of place in conjunction with the word "cancer" than it already does. But just as striking as the irony of my mom quitting smoking and bypassing the time frame where she had active risk factors and then developing lung cancer is the irony of being a transgender person facing the prospect of having to turn once more to a health care system that has not been kind, with a body that had, yet again, turned against me.

My reality is shaped differently from my mom's. Her medical complexities ultimately ended up saving her life. My medical complexities right now challenge mine, leave me in limbo, with a message of "you have a marker of cancer that can pop up months or even years before cancer itself shows, so just live with that knowledge and keep scheduling regular follow-ups."

Easier said than done.

LIFE, DEATH, REALITY, expression. If I had not chosen to change my gender, by way of surgery and hormones, perhaps I wouldn't have gone through two rounds of cancer testing in six months. If I hadn't taken the action of attempting suicide, twice, and been working for years with people aging and dying, I'm not sure I would be able to accept any of the messages or premonitions I seem to receive from the universe. If I wasn't transgender, I wouldn't have attempted suicide.

If I hadn't had the ensuing premonitions, I wouldn't have known to keep searching for my mom. To keep advocating. I wouldn't have known that in a way, we were traveling down similar paths, with what felt like a message from the universe trying to reconnect us.

I'd been keeping details from her about my fears of cancer. I didn't want anyone to worry about what might not be, or to think that the hormones are the cause and therefore think gender transition is not natural. I retreated from communication and kept quiet over the holidays, drawing a divide between myself and my family that was reminiscent of my younger, using years. Silence became my reality. Just as it had on social media.

But with my mom's diagnosis, that all changed. The fear of disclosure stopped, replaced instead by a calling to help support her through her road to recovery, to confide in her my own fears, share in hers, and reflect on the surreal timing of our independent encounters with cancer and complex medical scenarios. In a way, cancer has healed what was still fractured in our relationship and helped us bridge our gaps. It brought us back together in a way that a mother and daughter would typically bond and over a decidedly female-dominated topic, but that still brought sensitivity to my own gender in a respectful manner. She cares about me. She loves me. She doesn't want me to develop cancer, especially breast cancer, whether I'm a woman, a cisgender man, or a transgender man. Her being aware of my situation kept me accountable and forced me not to stick my head in the sand, but instead stare down the speed-bumped highway of my own flesh and veins.

Gender transition isn't a fairytale. There is no Neverland, no happily ever after. It's a serious and permanent life-changing event that carries with it serious risks and consequences. It also can heal wounds and breathe life into our lungs.

I pulled up a chair next to my mom's hospital bed and offered her ice cream. She picked at it a moment before shoving the long-handled spoon in it and pushing it aside. She pressed her head back into her pillow, tears welling up in her eyes.

I reached out and held her hand, weak from her body's fight and wrinkled from the onslaught of age. She squeezed, tears starting the slow trickle down her cheek. She told me how much she loved me. How proud she was of me for the man I'd become.

Then she told me to find a place in the patient freezer for her ice cream.

Acknowledgments

This book represents the culmination of one of the most challenging and time-consuming projects I've ever undertaken. It would be impossible to thank all the individuals and organizations that have helped make this book happen. To my mom, friends, peers, providers, and anyone else who has lent a hand or stood up for me along the way: thank you.

CPSIA information can be obtained
at www.ICGtesting.com
Printed in the USA
BVHW072004070119
537207BV00024B/3552/P